24.95

**Illustrators:**
Bruce Hedges
Ken Tunnel

**Editor:**
Janet Cain, M. Ed.

**Editorial Project Manager:**
Ina Massler Levin, M.A.

**Editor in Chief:**
Sharon Coan, M.S. Ed.

**Art Director:**
Elayne Roberts

**Art Coordination Assistant:**
Cheri Macoubrie Wilson

**Cover Artist:**
Denise Bauer

**Product Manager:**
Phil Garcia

**Imaging:**
James Edward Grace
Ralph Olmedo, Jr.

**Publishers:**
Rachelle Cracchiolo, M.S. Ed.
Mary Dupuy Smith, M.S. Ed.

# Storytime Activities to Help Children Cope

D1249741

**Author:**

*Grace Jasmine*

Teacher Created Materials

*Teacher Created Materials, Inc.*
6421 Industry Way
Westminster, CA 92683
**ISBN-1-57690-081-9**

*©1998 Teacher Created Materials, Inc.*          Made in U.S.A.

# Table of Contents

# Introduction

The goal of *Storytime Activities to Help Children Cope* is to make the job of early childhood educators easier by providing fresh ideas and strategies that allow teachers to do what they do best—create developmentally appropriate, positive learning environments for young children.

This book includes the following features:

- Section introductions that describe the issues addressed in this book. These issues include divorce, addiction, death and grief, having special needs, moving/new situations, tolerance, discrimination, loneliness, illness, and abuse.

- A specific table of contents at the beginning of each section describing what is included.

- Complete, illustrated, and reproducible stories that focus on some of the difficult issues children may face. Page 11 describes how to make books using the stories.

- Patterns that make it easy to create stick puppets and flannelboard pieces so young children can retell the stories or describe their own experiences and feelings. Page 12 describes how to make the puppets, flannelboard pieces, and some simple stages.

- A bibliography of children's books (page 10) that can be used to extend each coping theme.

- Complete activities that will help children learn a variety of coping strategies that they will use throughout their lives.

- Descriptions of the kinds of behaviors that teachers can expect from young children when the stories are being presented (pages 6–9).

- A list of materials and equipment (page 11) that is needed in order to make the stories into books and for children to complete the activities.

# Helping Children Cope

Adults who recognize their responsibility toward all children deeply want to help make their lives as easy and painless as possible. The reality is, however, that we cannot always keep bad things from happening to the children in our lives. What we can and must do is protect and care for children as best we can while teaching them strategies and skills they can use to protect and care for themselves.

Before we can teach children how to effectively deal with their problems and feelings, we must face our own feelings, accept them, and get help with them from other adults. Children are young people, not adults, and they do not experience the world as we do. To pass our adult feelings and fears on to children is to burden them unnecessarily.

Instead, we must listen to children and from them learn what they are struggling with. Otherwise, we risk going too far by providing information or raising issues that a child may neither want nor be ready to assimilate. Remember the story of the young girl who asked her mother where she came from. The conscientious mother dutifully and lovingly began to explain about love, conception, and birth only to have her daughter impatiently interrupt with the statement that her new friend comes from New York, and where did she come from?

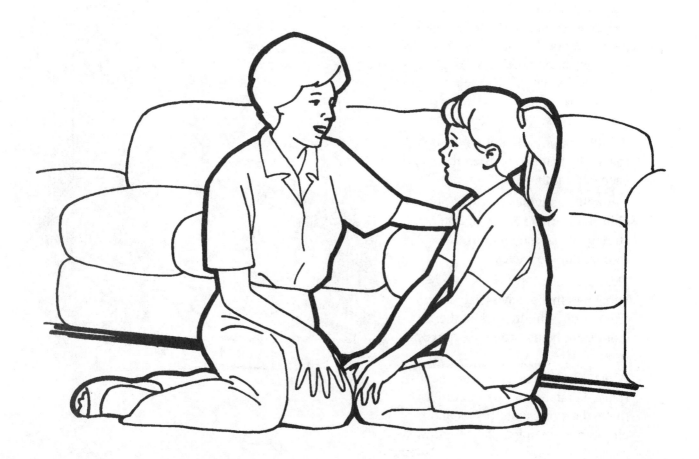

# Helping Children Cope *(cont.)*

*Storytime Activities to Help Children Cope* offers stories and activities that help you recognize problems children face, accept and acknowledge children's feelings, and empower children with ways they can learn to cope with physical and emotional adversity. Provide a supportive environment for children to share their feelings, and then approach the issues honestly and matter-of-factly. Withhold judgment and criticism and offer support and caring. Remember and respect the fact that we are all different.

Children learn best by doing, so provide many opportunities for children to role-play situations. Encourage children to share and participate in the activities, but do not force them. Youngsters also learn well by observing. Respect the boundaries and privacy of children who do not choose to participate by simply allowing them to watch. Insist that children show each other respect when they are around you, and reinforce that demand by setting a constant behavior example for them yourself.

# What to Expect

The coping stories included in *Storytime Activities to Help Children Cope* and the additional books suggested on page 10 can easily be presented in a structured setting such as circle time. Circle time gives children the opportunity to learn coping skills in a safe and supportive environment. The information shown below and on pages 7–9 will help you know what to expect from children ages two to five, during circle time.

## Toddling Two-Year-Olds

Two-year-olds are usually the youngest members of most circle time experiences. Toddlers have their own special needs, behaviors, and reactions to circle time.

The following list will give educators who work with these youngsters some guidelines for what is developmentally appropriate for toddling two-year-olds.

- Two-year-olds enjoy looking at colorful pictures. Simple pictures with easy-to-recognize objects are best.

- Simple stories with repetitive language work well with children who are just learning to speak and understand words. Two-year-olds will have difficulty attending to complicated, long, or wordy stories and discussions.

- Enthusiastic and fluent readers will captivate two-year-olds. Toddlers may not have a clear understanding of what you mean or the words you are using, but they are very aware of your tone of voice and the emotion behind the words you read.

- Two-year-olds have short attention spans. They might want to cuddle or sit in your lap while you are reading aloud. Circle time for toddlers can be a great opportunity for hugs and tender loving care.

- Do not be surprised if two-year-old students wander in and out of circle time and become involved in their own activities. Being aware of when to stop reading to two-year olds is just as important as making time to do the reading.

# What to Expect *(cont.)*

## Terrific Three-Year-Olds

Three-year-olds love creating their own stories as well as listening to stories told by others. They think books are wonderful. Because three-year-olds have minds of their own, they will let you know when they are through listening to a story.

The following list will give educators who work with these youngsters some guidelines for what is developmentally appropriate for terrific three-year-olds.

- Most three-year-olds will really appreciate hearing stories. In fact, they love to hear the same stories again and again. This kind of repetition is very helpful to them. They will begin to recognize words and start to use the kind of cognition that leads to reading comprehension.

- Three-year-olds, like all other people, have different temperaments as well as likes and dislikes. Some three-year-olds will have certain kinds of stories that they like best. They often enjoy funny stories and books that relate to the world as they see it. Most will have favorite books that they will request time after time. Be aware of and respect the children's preferences. Try ending circle time with a student's request for a favorite book.

- Some three-year-olds enjoy looking at books alone, but most prefer to have someone read to them. These youngsters enjoy the special and undivided attention of an adult who is reading aloud.

- Three-year-olds need to be taught how to handle books, and they need to be lovingly reminded again and again.

- Involve three-year-olds in setting up the circle time area in your classroom. Let them feel that they are helping you make a special place for circle time.

# What to Expect *(cont.)*

## Fearless Four-Year-Olds

Four-year-olds are really feeling grown up. They test themselves as well as the adults around them. They make friends easily and enjoy interacting. They are beginning to be able to work cooperatively in groups. Four-year-olds like school. They are becoming increasingly verbal and creative.

The following list will give educators who work with these youngsters some guidelines for what is developmentally appropriate for fearless four-year-olds.

- Four-your-olds will test their limits. They may express a great deal of interest or none at all. Be prepared for honest feedback to your circle time story selections.
- Four-year-olds will enjoy role-playing and retelling the stories.
- Four-year-olds who have been read to may recognize words that they have heard and seen again and again. Some four-year-olds will want to learn to read, while others will not show any interest in the words on the page.
- Four-year-olds live active, fast-paced lives. They can use circle time to settle down and regroup. Make it relaxing for everyone and set flexible standards.
- Four-year-olds will enjoy saying the lines from familiar books with you as you read them aloud. Encourage these youngsters to get involved in the exciting parts of the stories.

# What to Expect *(cont.)*

## Fabulous Five-Year-Olds

Five-year-olds who have moved into a regular kindergarten from a preschool sometimes regress as they adjust to a new situation. Children who have not been in school before the age of five may be overwhelmed by being around so many children at once. However, it will not be long before they begin to enjoy making friends. Five-year-olds are intensely curious about the world around them.

The following list will give educators who work with these youngsters some guidelines for what is developmentally appropriate for fabulous five-year-olds.

- Five-year-olds enjoy being in groups and interacting. They are interested in the way things should be done, and they like to do things correctly. They like to know what the rules are and usually try to follow them. They also want other people to follow the rules. They monitor the behavior of others and are sometimes tattletales.

- Five-year-olds usually enjoy being read to and have an increasing understanding of what they hear. They are constantly improving their ability to verbalize their thoughts and opinions.

- Five-year-olds are often overwhelmed by new situations and can be intimidated by too many new things. They frequently find themselves in totally new situations in which they have no idea what the expectations are. Circle time can be used to help them understand the amazing number of new experiences they encounter daily.

- Five-year-olds still need plenty of tender loving care and affection.

- Five-year-olds can be very helpful. They can perform simple tasks and usually take a great deal of pride in being chosen as helpers.

# Books to Read Aloud

## Divorce

Brown, Laurene Krasny & Marc. *Dinosaurs Divorce.* Little, Brown & Company, 1986.
Porter-Gaylord, Laurel. *I Love My Daddy Because...; I Love My Mommy Because....* Dutton, 1991.
Rogers, Fred. *Let's Talk About It: Divorce.* Putnam, 1996.

## Addiction

Berenstain, Stan & Jan. *The Berenstain Bears and the Drug Free Zone.* Random, 1993.
Super, Gretchen. *What Are Drugs?* Twenty-First Century Books, 1990.
Vigna, Judith. *I Wish Daddy Didn't Drink So Much.* Albert Whitman, 1988.

## Death and Grief

Carson, Jo. *You Hold Me and I'll Hold You.* Franklin Watts, 1992.
Viorst, Judith. *The Tenth Good Thing About Barney.* Antheneum, 1971.

## Tolerance

Berenstain, Stan & Jan. *The Berenstain Bears' New Neighbors.* Random, 1994.
Bunting, Eve. *Fly Away Home.* Houghton Mifflin, 1991.

## Specially-Abled

Berenstain, Stan & Jan. *The Berenstain Bears and the Wheelchair Commando.* Random, 1993.
Martin, Bill Jr. and John Archambault. *Knots on a Counting Rope.* Holt, 1987.

## Moving/New Situations

Aliki. *Welcome, Little Baby.* Simon, 1988.
Greenwood, Pamela D. *What About My Goldfish?* Houghton Mifflin, 1993.
Harshman, Marc. *Moving Days.* Cobblehill, 1994.

## Loneliness

Barrett, Joyce Durham. *Willie's Not the Hugging Kind.* HarperCollins, 1989.
Sharmat, Marjorie Weinman. *The 329th Friend.* Macmillan, 1992.

## Illness

Breebaart, Joeri & Piet. *When I Die, Will I Get Better?* Peter Bedrick Books, 1993.
Butler, Daphne. *First Look in the Hospital.* Gareth Stevens, 1991.
Rogers, Fred. *Going to the Doctor.* Putnam, 1986.

## Abuse

Berenstain, Stan & Jan. *The Berenstain Bears Learn About Strangers.* Random, 1985.
Brady, Janeen. *Safety Kids Personal Safety* (cassette and book). Brite Music Inc., 1984.
Wachter, Oralee. *No More Secrets for Me.* Little, Brown & Company, 1994.

# Making the Book Work for You

*Storytime Activities to Help Children Cope* has nine stories relating to these important issues: divorce, addiction, death, tolerance, special needs, moving, loneliness, illness, and abuse. In conjunction with the stories a variety of easy-to-use activities are suggested. Patterns for the stories and activities are provided. Many of the supplies and equipment needed to prepare and use the units in this book are things you probably already have. These include the following:

- Access to a copier
- White copier paper
- Art supplies such as crayons and markers
- Gift wrapping supplies
- Tape and nontoxic white glue
- Safety scissors and adult scissors
- Hole puncher
- Stapler
- Ruler and yardstick
- Laminator and laminating film or clear contact paper
- Poster board and construction paper
- Manila envelopes
- Old shirts and smocks
- Poster paint and paintbrushes
- Paper towels, sponges, and other clean-up supplies
- Craft sticks
- Ribbon, yarn, and/or string

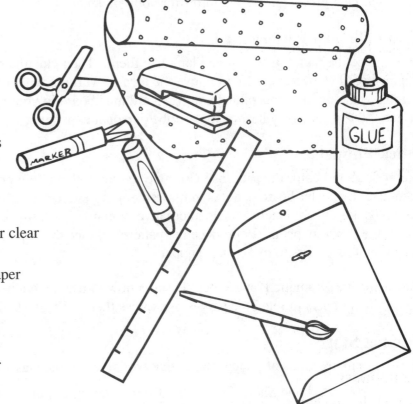

## Nine Stories in One Book

The stories in *Storytime Activities to Help Children Cope* have been designed with the idea that each student will have his or her own copy of every story. This way students can color the illustrations and take the books home to read again and again.

When preparing a unit, reproduce the cover and all of the story pages. Be sure to make enough copies so that each student in your class gets a story book. Then collate and staple each set of pages. Allow students to color the illustrations in their books. You may wish to make an extra copy for the classroom library. For the class copy, color the illustrations, laminate and trim the pages, punch holes, and place the book in a three-ring binder.

# Stick Puppet and Flannelboard Patterns

## Ready-to-Use Patterns

*Storytime Activities to Help Children Cope* provides you with character patterns for the coping stories. You can use these patterns to create stick puppets and flannelboard pieces. The patterns will save you time and be a great source of comfort for your students.

## Flannelboard Patterns

Reproduce the patterns. Color and laminate them. Then glue them onto pieces of felt to make flannelboard characters. Children love the idea of working with a flannelboard, and it is an easy way to reinforce the main events of a story. Keep a flannelboard in your circle time area. Children can use it to retell the stories they hear or to describe personal experiences.

## Stick Puppets

Reproduce and color the patterns. Use glue to mount them onto poster board. You may wish to laminate the poster board patterns to make them more durable. Then glue or tape a craft stick or ruler to the back of each pattern. As an alternative, you may wish to create a Puppet Center so students can make their own puppets. Reproduce the patterns. Place the copies and some art supplies in the center. Then invite students to make their puppets.

Introduce the Dramatic Play Center. Discuss how to use the puppets in the center. Encourage students to use the puppets to retell the stories or express their feelings about their own experiences.

## Puppet Stages

There are many kinds of puppet stages that work well in the classroom.

- Curtain Rod and Sheet: From a hardware store, get a curtain rod or wooden dowel rod that is 6' (1.8 m) long. Hem one end of a twin-size flat sheet, and put it on the rod. Hang the rod over two chairs or anywhere that is convenient. This type of stage can be constructed quickly and is easy to store.

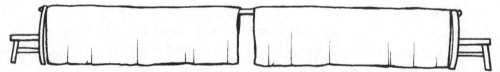

- Large Cardboard Carton: Obtain an appliance cardboard box from a store, cut a hole in the front, and decorate it. This type of stage is fun to use but can be difficult to store.

- Science Presentation Board: Buy a tri-fold science presentation board from any teacher supply store. Cut a square in the upper half of the board's middle section. Place the board so the two sides point towards the back. Then decorate it with paper or paint. You will actually be using the wrong side of the board. This type of stage folds up and can be easily stored.

# Divorce

## Section Introduction

Coping with Divorce (page 14)

## Story

"Why My Daddy Left" (pages 15–27)

This story presents the issue of divorce in a manner that is developmentally appropriate for young children. It shows the different emotions that children might feel if their parents are getting or have gotten a divorce and reassures them that they are not to blame.

## Stick Puppet and Flannelboard Patterns

These patterns (pages 28–32) can be used to help children understand the issues that are emphasized in the story.

## Activities

All of these activities support children who are having to cope with divorce by recognizing and addressing their feelings and concerns in a positive, relaxed atmosphere.

# Coping with Divorce

## Helping Children Understand

You can help children who are dealing with divorce by clarifying many misconceptions that they may have. Their self-confidence and coping skills will improve as you address the following issues:

1. Children are not responsible for their parents getting divorced. Adults get divorced because they have problems with their relationships that they are not able to solve.

2. Divorce does not cause parents to stop loving their children. Because divorce is a stressful time for adults, they may forget to express love to their children.

3. Mothers, fathers, or guardians will continue to care for the children after the divorce. Many children are afraid that they will be abandoned because of the divorce. They worry that no one will be left to take care of them.

4. Divorce causes families to change or be different than they once were. However, this does not mean that the families are destroyed. Children of divorced parents may also have to adjust to other changes, such as moving or financial struggles, as a result of the divorce.

5. Children can have happy, normal lives even if they only get to see one of their parents. After the divorce, life usually improves for these families since the adults are calmer and happier.

6. Divorce happens to all kinds of children. It does not mean that the children are bad if their parents get divorced.

7. It is important for children to tell how they feel about divorce. Then adults, such as teachers, counselors, and parents, can help them deal with those feelings. Problems usually seem more manageable if other people provide children with the emotional support they need.

8. It is not likely that divorced parents will get back together again. However, parents sometimes make new friends and remarry.

9. Divorce can cause children to feel many different emotions, including anger, guilt, sadness, confusion, and loneliness. These kinds of feelings are very normal.

10. Children cannot make their parents get back together, and they are not responsible for solving adult problems.

11. Children can love both parents even though they only live with one of them.

12. Children can learn to cope with the divorce of their parents and grow up to be well-adjusted adults.

## In This Book

This book provides a variety of suggestions to help children deal with experiences relating to divorce. The section begins with a story about a father leaving the family home because of a divorce (pages 15–27). Stick puppet and flannel board patterns (pages 28–32) are provided for children to role-play the story as well as their own experiences, fears, and concerns. Activities (pages 33–42) are included to help children understand and cope with divorce.

# Why My Daddy Left

My mommy and daddy are getting a divorce. This means they won't be married anymore. They said they do not want to live together, so my daddy moved out of our house. Now he has an apartment on the other side of town. I get to see him on weekends and sometimes on holidays.

My mommy and daddy used to love each other, but now they don't. Before my daddy left, he and my mommy often yelled and said mean things to each other.

Sometimes it seemed like they were mad at me when they were really mad at each other. This made me feel sad.

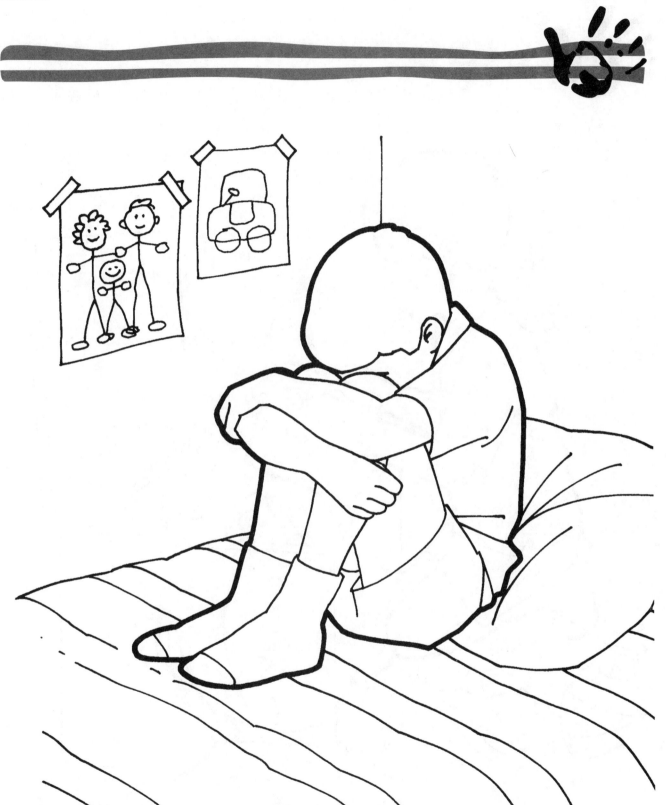

I am sad that my parents are getting a divorce.
Sometimes I cry about it. Other times I get mad. I
really wish my daddy lived with me all the time. I would
like to be with him every day.

For awhile I was scared. I thought my mommy and daddy were getting divorced because of me. I tried to be extra good. It didn't help.

20

I told my mommy this, and she hugged me. She said, "Daddy and I aren't getting divorced because of you. I love you just the same, and I know your daddy does too!"

My daddy also says he loves me just as much as ever. I believe him, too. Now I know that the divorce has nothing to do with me or how much he loves me.

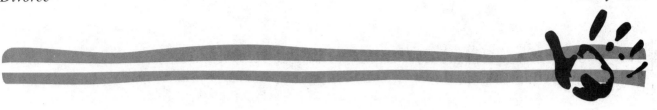

It has been three months since my mommy and daddy got divorced. Mommy isn't as mad at Daddy anymore. Daddy isn't as mad at Mommy anymore. Now my daddy and mommy don't yell when they see each other.

I go with my mommy to meetings for single parents and their kids. Sometimes they have hay rides, carnivals, and bowling. That is fun. We meet some nice people and make new friends.

Now I know that my mommy and daddy aren't the only parents who have gotten divorced.

Even though my mommy and daddy are divorced, I still have both of them. They love me just as much as ever. They are much happier, and I have a lot more fun with them.

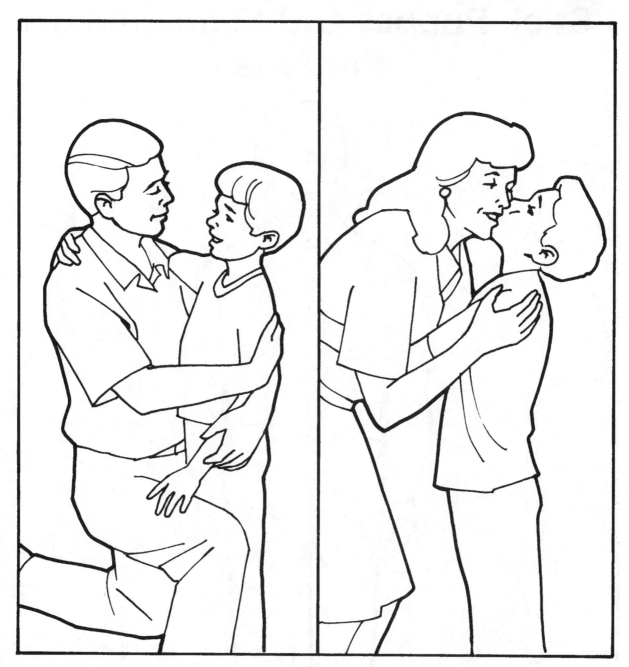

Sometimes I still feel sad that my mommy and daddy are divorced. But most of the time I'm happy because I know that they will always love me and take care of me. I know that Mommy and Daddy will always want to be with me.

# Stick Puppet and Flannelboard Patterns

**Daddy**

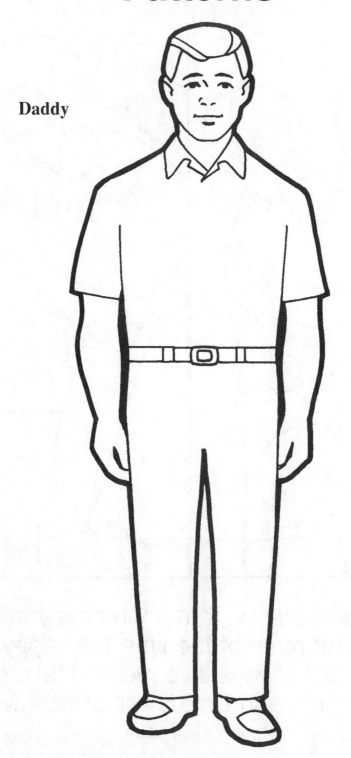

# Stick Puppet and Flannelboard Patterns *(cont.)*

**Mommy**

# Stick Puppet and Flannelboard Patterns *(cont.)*

**Boy**

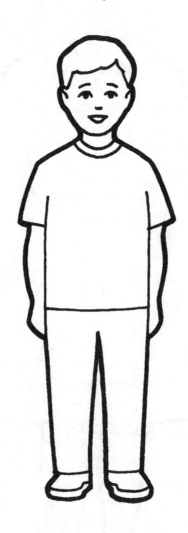

# Stick Puppet and Flannelboard Patterns *(cont.)*

**Daddy's Apartment**

# Stick Puppet and Flannelboard Patterns *(cont.)*

## Mommy's House

# Visit Calendar

## Purpose:

The purpose of this activity is to give young children a tangible way to make the time between visits with divorced parents seem more real and manageable by having them make Visit Calendars.

## Preparation Time: One hour

## What You Need:

- Calendar (page 34)
- Pens
- Scissors
- Drawing materials
- Glue
- Construction paper
- One-hole punch
- Ribbon or yarn

**Calendar**

| Sunday | Monday | Tuesday | Wednesday | Thursday | Friday | Saturday |
|--------|--------|---------|-----------|----------|--------|----------|
|  |  | ★ |  |  |  |  |
|  |  |  | ★ |  |  |  |
|  |  |  |  |  | ★ |  |
|  |  | ★ |  |  |  |  |
|  |  |  |  |  |  |  |

## What to Do:

Young children who are experiencing the aftermath of divorce often have a difficult time understanding when they will see the absent parent again and the number of days that will pass between visits. Many children will not have had much exposure to calendars. However, calendars provide an excellent way for them to keep track of the passage of time. As children become accustomed to counting the days from one visit to the next, this will help ease their concerns.

Before doing this activity, reproduce and prepare a calendar (page 34) for each participating child. Show a variety of different calendars. Point out that calendars can come in many different shapes and sizes but they are all used to show the passage of days and months. Give students their calendars. Explain how a calendar works. Help the children mark the dates they want on their calendars. Most children will enjoy starting with the birth dates of family members. Then tell them that they can mark any other important dates, such as parental visits, on their calendars. Invite students to decorate their calendars.

Send the calendars home with notes asking parents to help mark the dates that are important to their children.

## What to Say:

Today we are going to learn about calendars. Can anyone tell me what a calendar is? Have you ever used a calendar to see how many days or months it would be until your birthday or until a holiday? Let's look at some different calendars. How are these calendars alike? How are they different? Now look at the calendar I gave you. I will tell you how it works. There are twelve months in a year. Let's count to twelve. Now I will tell you the name of each month and something interesting about it.

# Calendar

| Sunday | Monday | Tuesday | Wednesday | Thursday | Friday | Saturday |
|--------|--------|---------|-----------|----------|--------|----------|
|        |        |         |           |          |        |          |
|        |        |         |           |          |        |          |
|        |        |         |           |          |        |          |
|        |        |         |           |          |        |          |
|        |        |         |           |          |        |          |

# What I Like to Do with Mommy

## Purpose:

The purpose of this activity is to give young children the opportunity to make picture books that show the activities they like to do with their mothers.

## Preparation Time: One hour

## What You Need:

- Fun with Mommy (page 36), several copies per child
- Various art supplies such as crayons, colored pencils, markers, glue, and glitter
- Three-hole punch
- Ribbon or yarn
- Construction paper

## What to Do:

Use the following activities (pages 35–38) to reinforce the positive and loving feelings children have toward their mothers. Have children complete the activities on pages 39–42 to give students opportunities to express the same feelings toward their fathers. The books and love notes that the children make will be special gifts for their mothers and fathers, regardless of which parent is the primary caregiver.

Begin this activity by reproducing page 36, making several copies per child. Create a sample book for students to examine. Ask children to make several pictures of things they like to do with their mothers. Then place the pictures between two pieces of construction paper. Punch holes along the left-hand side of the pages and the cover. Use ribbon or yarn to bind the books. Allow children to decorate the covers of their picture books. You may wish to ask students to dictate sentences to tell about their pictures. Write the sentences on the appropriate pages.

## What to Say:

Today you are going to make a special picture book for your mommy. You will get to draw pictures and make a cover for your book. Then I will help you bind it, or put it together, using ribbon or yarn. This is what your book will look like when you are finished. *(Display the sample book.)* Each of you will make a book about two special people, you and your mommy! Let's talk about some of the things you like to do with your mommy. Who can think of something he or she likes to do with his or her mommy? *(Encourage students to brainstorm a list of things they like to do with their mothers.)*

# Fun with Mommy

# A Love Note to Mommy

## Purpose:

The purpose of this activity is to give young children the opportunity to communicate in writing the feelings they have for their mothers.

## Preparation Time: One hour

## What You Need:

- Heavy paper or cardstock
- My Love Note to Mommy (page 38), one copy per child
- Pens or pencils
- Crayons or markers
- Envelopes
- Postage stamps
- Stickers such as hearts or flowers (optional)
- List or database of mothers' addresses

## What to Do:

During a divorce it is important to reinforce children's feelings of love for each parent. In this activity, you will help children write love notes to their mothers.

Before this activity, gather together the materials. Be sure to have postage stamps available since children will want to be assured that their notes will be mailed.

Reproduce page 38 on heavy paper or cardstock, making one copy per child. Cut out and fold the copies to make note cards. Begin this activity by telling children that they are going to write love notes to their mothers. Most children will need to dictate the notes as you write them. You may wish to enlist the help of adult volunteers or older students for writing the notes. After the notes are written, encourage the children to illustrate them. Place the notes in envelopes. Show children how to seal their envelopes. Allow them to watch you address the envelopes. Then ask children to help you place the stamps on the envelopes. They may wish to put heart or flower stickers on the seals of their envelopes. Make a point of taking children to a nearby mailbox even if it is the one in the school office. Allow children to mail their letters.

## What to Say:

Today you are going to write a special love note to your mommy. I will help you write what you would like to say to your mommy. When you are done writing the note, you can draw pictures on it. Then I will address the envelope for you. You will get to seal the envelope and put a stamp on it. Then we will take a walk to a mailbox. You will get to mail your love note to your mommy. In a couple of days, your mommy will open up her mailbox and have a special note from you telling her how much you love her.

# My Love Note to Mommy

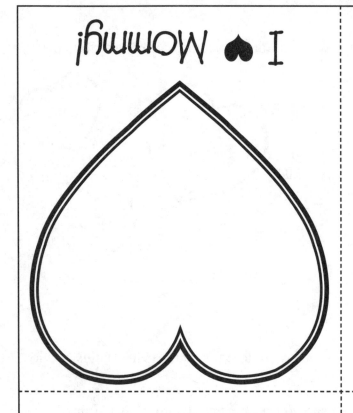

I ♥ Mommy!

Fold 1

Fold 2

Dear Mommy,

_____

_____

_____

_____

_____

_____

_____

Love,

_____

# What I Like to Do with Daddy

## Purpose:

The purpose of this activity is to give young children the opportunity to make picture books that show the activities they like to do with their fathers.

## Preparation Time: One hour

## What You Need:

- Fun with Daddy (page 40), several copies per child

- Various art supplies such as crayons, colored pencils, markers, glue, and glitter

- Three-hole punch

- Ribbon or yarn

- Construction paper

## What to Do:

Use the following activities (pages 39–42) to reinforce the positive and loving feelings children have toward their fathers. The books and love notes that the children make will be special gifts for their fathers, regardless of which parent is the primary caregiver.

Begin this activity by reproducing page 40, making several copies per child. Create a sample book for students to examine. Ask children to make several pictures of things they like to do with their fathers. Then place the pictures between two pieces of construction paper. Punch holes along the left-hand side of the pages and the cover. Use ribbon or yarn to bind the books. Allow children to decorate the covers of their picture books. You may wish to ask students to dictate sentences to tell about their pictures. Write the sentences on the appropriate pages.

## What to Say:

Today you are going to make a special picture book for your daddy. You will get to draw pictures and make a cover for your book. Then I will help you bind it, or put it together, using ribbon or yarn. This is what your book will look like when you are finished. *(Display the sample book.)* Each of you will make a book about two special people, you and your daddy! Let's talk about some of the things you like to do with your daddy. Who can think of something he or she likes to do with his or her daddy? *(Encourage students to brainstorm a list of things they like to do with their fathers.)*

# Fun with Daddy

# A Love Note to Daddy

## Purpose:
The purpose of this activity is to give young children the opportunity to communicate in writing the feelings they have for their fathers.

## Preparation Time: One hour

## What You Need:
- Heavy paper or cardstock
- My Love Note to Daddy (page 42), one copy per child
- Pens or pencils
- Crayons or markers
- Envelopes
- Postage stamps
- Stickers such as hearts (optional)
- List or database of fathers' addresses

## What to Do:
During a divorce it is important to reinforce children's feeling of love for each parent. In this activity, you will help children write love notes to their fathers.

Before this activity, gather together the materials. Be sure to have postage stamps available since children will want to be assured that their notes will be mailed.

Reproduce page 42 on heavy paper or cardstock, making one copy per child. Cut out and fold the copies to make note cards. Begin this activity by telling children that they are going to write love notes to their fathers. Most children will need to dictate the notes as you write them. You may wish to enlist the help of adult volunteers or older students for writing the notes. After the notes are written, encourage the children to illustrate them. Place the notes in envelopes. Show children how to seal their envelopes. Allow them to watch you address the envelopes. Then ask children to help you place the stamps on the envelopes. They may wish to put heart stickers on the seals of their envelopes. Make a point of taking children to a nearby mailbox even if it is the one in the school office. Allow children to mail their letters.

## What to Say:
Today you are going to write a special love note to your daddy. I will help you write what you would like to say to your daddy. When you are done writing the note, you can draw pictures on it. Then I will address the envelope for you. You will get to seal the envelope and put a stamp on it. Then we will take a walk to a mailbox. You will get to mail your love note to your daddy. In a couple of days, your daddy will open up his mailbox and have a special note from you telling him how much you love him.

# My Love Note to Daddy

I ♥ Daddy!

Fold 1

Fold 2

Dear Daddy,

_____

_____

_____

_____

_____

_____

_____

_____

Love,

_____

# Addiction

## Section Introduction

Saying No to Drugs (page 44)

## Story

"Little Bird Says, 'No!' " (page 45–52)

This story shows children how to make good choices when someone they know or a stranger offers drugs to them. It points out that drugs are harmful to the body.

## Stick Puppet and Flannelboard Patterns

These patterns (pages 53–57) can be used to help children understand the issues that are emphasized in the story.

## Activities

- What I Like About Me (pages 58 and 59)

- Yell! Run! Tell! (pages 60 and 61)

- Mini-Talent Show (page 62)

- Writing Praise Letters (pages 63–65)

- What Should You Do? (pages 66–71)

All of these activities reinforce ways to avoid addictive behaviors by developing children's self-awareness, self-esteem, and decision-making skills.

# Saying No to Drugs

## What Are Drugs?

Drugs can be legal or illegal chemicals that change how the brain and body work. Drugs include alcohol, tobacco, marijuana, narcotics, stimulants, depressants, hallucinogens, and inhalants. It is important for children to realize that all medicines are drugs. However, medicines that are used correctly can help people who are sick. Point out that they should only take medicines if these are given to them by their doctors or parents.

## Self-Concept

Educators have noted that children who do not use drugs usually have good self-images and like who they are. To promote a positive self-concept, help children realize that they are important people, their families and friends love them, they have the power to make good choices, and they can influence others in positive ways. Help children discover ways that they can believe in themselves. Role-play a variety of scenarios so they will know what to do when someone offers to give them drugs. Discuss how true friends would never ask them to do something that could be harmful. Remind children to tell a trusted adult if someone tries to sell or give them drugs.

## Why Do Some Children Use Drugs?

There are many reasons why some children get involved with potentially addictive substances. Listed below are just a few examples.

1. The child's friends use drugs. The child does not want to be left out or criticized by his/her friends.

2. A family member uses drugs. Sometimes adults will smoke, drink alcohol, or take pills to deal with the stress of everyday life. They do not realize that by doing this, they may unintentionally be condoning the use of drugs.

3. Drugs may make the child feel happier. However, the effects are only temporary. Many drug users will feel sadder and more depressed after they come down from the "high" feeling.

4. Advertisements convince adults as well as children that using drugs, such as cigarettes and alcohol, will be fun and make them more popular.

5. Some children use drugs as a form of rebellion against their parents or rules in general.

6. Some children are curious and decide to experiment with drugs just to see what it is like. They do not realize that using a drug just once may lead to addiction and a life-long habit or even death.

## In This Book

This book provides a variety of suggestions to help children deal with the potential dangers of drugs. The section begins with a story (pages 45–52) about a little bird who shows children how to say no to people who might try to get them to take drugs. Stick puppet and flannel board patterns (pages 53–57) are provided for children to role-play the story as well as their own experiences, fears, and concerns. Activities (pages 58–71) are included to help children have positive self-images so they will have the strength to refuse drugs.

# Little Bird Says, "No!"

Little Bird went outside to play.  Some older birds she knew from school came over to talk to her.  They were smoking cigarettes.

The older birds asked Little Bird to try a cigarette. One of them told her that she would feel grown up if she smoked.

Little Bird said, "No!"

One of the older birds called her a baby. But she did not care. She knew that smoking would hurt her body. She went inside to tell her mother. The older birds got scared and flew away. Little Bird's mother told her that she had done the right thing.

The next day, Little Bird walked down the street to play with her bunny friends.  At first they had a good time playing ball.

Soon Little Bird's bunny friends got tired of playing ball. They asked her if she wanted to do something much more fun. Little Bird asked what they wanted to do. One of the bunnies took out a jar of paint. He said that he and his sister like to sniff the paint. The bunny told Little Bird that it makes them feel happy and silly.

Little Bird knew that sniffing paint would hurt her brain, so she said, "No!"

She flew back to her house and told her father what happened. Her father thanked her for making such a good choice.

50

Then one day Little Bird was walking home from school with her best friend, Yellow Bird. Suddenly a stranger drove up next to them. Both Little Bird and Yellow Bird stepped away from the car because they knew they should never talk to strangers. This person looked very nice and was friendly. She offered the birds some pills.

Little Bird and Yellow Bird yelled, "No!" They both ran to Little Bird's house. They told Little Bird's parents what happened.

Little Bird's mother and father were proud that the children remembered what to do when they saw a stranger. They were glad that Little Bird and Yellow Bird were safe. Then they all jumped in the car and took Yellow Bird home.

52

# Stick Puppet and Flannelboard Patterns

**Little Bird**　　　　　　　　　　**Yellow Bird**

# Stick Puppet and Flannelboard Patterns *(cont.)*

**Little Bird's Mother**

**Little Bird's Father**

# Stick Puppet and Flannelboard Patterns *(cont.)*

### Older Birds

# Stick Puppet and Flannelboard Patterns *(cont.)*

**Boy and Girl Bunny Friends**

# Stick Puppet and Flannelboard Patterns *(cont.)*

### Stranger in a Car

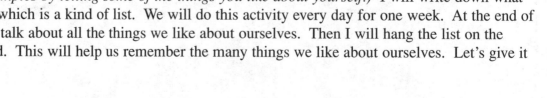

# What I Like About Me

## Purpose:

This activity fosters a positive self-image which plays an important part in helping children say no to drugs.

## Preparation Time: 15 minutes

## What You Need:

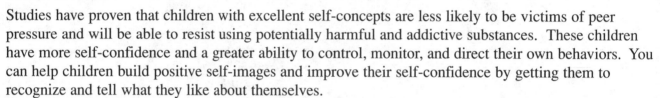

- What I Like About Myself Log (page 59)
- Pen or pencil
- Clipboard

## What to Do:

Studies have proven that children with excellent self-concepts are less likely to be victims of peer pressure and will be able to resist using potentially harmful and addictive substances. These children have more self-confidence and a greater ability to control, monitor, and direct their own behaviors. You can help children build positive self-images and improve their self-confidence by getting them to recognize and tell what they like about themselves.

Prepare for this activity by reproducing the log (page 59) so you can keep a daily record of how children respond to the sentence starter, "What I like about myself is . . . ."

Begin this activity by discussing with children some of the things they like about themselves. Children may describe a variety of things such as physical characteristics, personality traits, or special skills or possessions. Model the behavior by telling some of the things that you like about yourself. Then explain to the children that each day during circle time you will ask them to tell one thing that they like about themselves. Accept all responses without making judgments. Point out that you will write what they say on a log. Repeat this activity every day for one week. Display the log on a wall or bulletin board.

## What to Say:

We are going to do a new activity during circle time. It's really easy and everybody gets a turn. Please remember to be good listeners while someone else is talking. This is how we will do the activity. I want each of you to say one thing you like about yourself. Here are some things I like about myself. *(Provide some examples by telling some of the things you like about yourself.)* I will write down what you say on a log, which is a kind of list. We will do this activity every day for one week. At the end of the week, we will talk about all the things we like about ourselves. Then I will hang the list on the wall/bulletin board. This will help us remember the many things we like about ourselves. Let's give it a try.

# What I Like About Myself Log

| Date | Child's Name | What I like about myself is . . . |
|------|--------------|-----------------------------------|
|      |              |                                   |
|      |              |                                   |
|      |              |                                   |
|      |              |                                   |
|      |              |                                   |
|      |              |                                   |
|      |              |                                   |
|      |              |                                   |
|      |              |                                   |

# Yell! Run! Tell!

## Purpose:

This activity gives children the opportunity to role-play what they should do if someone offers drugs to them. It is important to practice these skills so they will be prepared. Then children use sequence cards to show their parents what they have learned about saying no to drugs.

## Preparation Time: 15 minutes

## What You Need:

- Heavy paper or cardstock
- Sequence Cards (page 61), one set per child
- Scissors or paper cutter
- Crayons or markers
- Laminating film (optional)
- Envelopes (optional)

## What to Do:

Explain to children that someday someone might offer drugs to them. This person could be an adult or another child. It might be someone they know or a stranger. It might even be a family member, a neighbor, or someone they think of as a friend. Be sure to discuss with children that they should never talk to strangers, no matter how nice or friendly they seem to be.

Then present facts about what drugs are and how they harm the body. Stress that medicines that are used correctly can help people who are sick. Remind children that it is all right to take medicines given to them by their doctors or parents. Tell children that drugs can include pills, anything that is smoked, such as cigarettes or marijuana, alcohol, and inhalants. Show them inhalants such as glue, paint, and correction fluid. Point out that some people use these products for something other than their intended purpose. Explain that they sniff the fumes to make themselves feel happy without thinking about how it hurts their brains.

Allow children to role-play how to say no, run away, and tell a trusted adult when someone tries to give drugs to them. Then provide copies of the sequence cards for children to take home and share what they have learned with their parents. You may wish to invite the children to color the cards. Then the cards can be laminated and sent home in the envelopes.

## What to Say:

Today you are going to practice what you will do if someone offers you some drugs. *(Model how to yell, "No," run away, and tell a trusted adult. Be sure each child gets a turn.)* Now that you are done, I will give you three cards to color and take home. You can put them in the correct order and show your parents what you have learned about saying no to drugs.

# Sequence Cards

## YELL!

## RUN!

## TELL!

# Mini-Talent Show

## Purpose:

This activity helps children develop self-confidence as well as recognize and use their talents. It also encourages children to feel comfortable expressing themselves in front of a group. These skills will help children be better prepared to resist potentially addictive substances.

## Preparation: One afternoon

## What You Need:

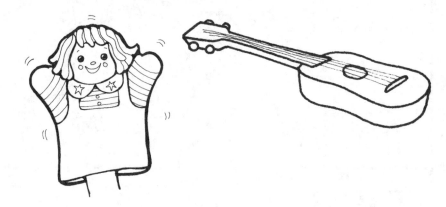

- Costumes—clothes, shoes, and accessories
- Musical instruments
- Puppets
- Video camera (optional)

## What to Do:

In this activity, children create and perform their own mini-talent show. It will give children an improved sense of self-worth and self-confidence when they perform and receive positive feedback from the group. Prepare for this activity by collecting a variety of clothing, shoes, and accessories that students can use as costumes. The costumes do not have to be expensive or elaborate. Garage sales can be a good source for these items. You may also wish to ask parents to send donations. Place the costumes in a box for easy storage. An old sheet or shower curtain may be used to create a stage. If you have a circle time area, you may wish to make this space available to the performers.

Explain to children that they are going to show the class their talents. Point out that everyone will get a chance to perform. Provide musical instruments, puppets, or anything else you think children might like to use. Tell children they can do any kind of presentation for the show. Be sure they feel safe performing in front of the group by emphasizing appropriate audience behavior. This will ensure that they have positive experiences during this activity. When discussing how to be a good audience member, show children how to applaud for each other's acts. Be sure to applaud loudly to give children a chance to realize that they have done a good job.

You may wish to videotape the talent show so the children can see themselves perform.

## What to Say:

We are going to have a talent show. Everyone will get to perform. You may wear costumes if you like. You may wish to use puppets, play musical instruments, dance, sing, or tell jokes. Remember that you need to be good audience members and clap after each performance. Let's practice clapping. (*Model appropriate audience behavior.*) Now you will need to decide what you will do for the show.

# Writing Praise Letters

## Purpose:

The purpose of this activity is to help children recognize their value and to provide positive feedback for good behavior. Children receive praise letters from teachers, other school personnel, and parents.

## Preparation Time: One hour

## What You Need:

- Praise Letter (page 64)
- Praise Letter Mailbox (page 65)
- Letter-size envelopes

## What to Do:

Using written praise for children is a tangible way of letting them know you appreciate their good qualities and behaviors. Begin this activity by writing some sample letters and creating the Praise Letter Mailbox (page 65). This mailbox will provide a special place in your classroom for the letters your children receive.

Begin by explaining what praise is. Then describe how a Praise Letter (page 64) can be used to tell someone some good things about him or herself. Show the children the sample letters that you have written. Point out the mailbox that you have created. Tell them that this special mailbox will be for the letters they receive from you.

Pick a child to be the mail carrier once each week. You may wish to choose a specific time of day to allow this child to deliver the mail. During circle time, help each child read aloud his or her letter to provide the additional positive reinforcement in front of the group.

Send notes home to parents and blank copies of the Praise Letter. Encourage parents to send letters to their children, praising them for things they have done at home.

## What to Say:

I have made a mailbox for our classroom. It's for letters that you are going to get. These letters are called "praise letters." Praise is when someone tells you that you have done a good job or that you have done something special. Who can think of something that they have gotten praise for? *(Allow children to give examples of times they have received praise.)* Here are some examples of praise letters that I have written. *(Share the sample letters.)* Once each week, I will pick one of you to be our mail carrier. The mail carrier's job will be to deliver the letters. Then I will help you read aloud your praise letters. Who would like to be our first mail carrier? *(Select a volunteer.)*

# Praise Letter

Date _____

Dear _____,

You are a special child.  I am proud of you because:

❑ _____

_____

❑ _____

_____

❑ _____

_____

❑ _____

_____

Sincerely,

_____
Teacher

_____
School

# Praise Letter Mailbox

## Materials:

- Large file box with lid
- Construction paper or contact paper
- Scissors
- Glue

## Directions:

1. Remove the lid from the box. Cover the outside of the box and the lid with construction paper. As an alternative you may wish to use contact paper.

2. Glue on decorations such as hearts and smiley faces. Allow the glue to dry.

3. Use scissors to make a letter-sized slit in the middle, top side of the lid.

4. Place the lid back on the box.

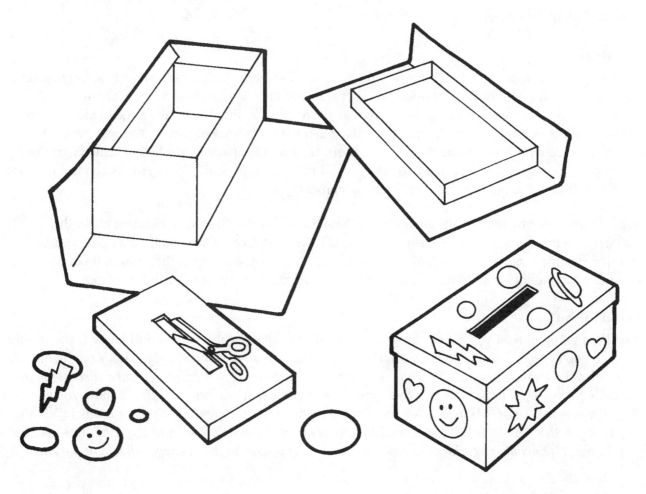

# What Should You Do?

## Purpose:
This activity helps students learn to make good decisions using a variety of scenarios that show ways that children may be offered drugs.

## Preparation Time: Several hours

## What You Need:

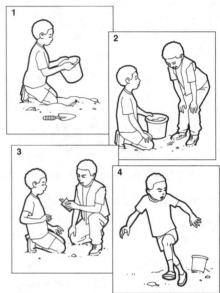

- "Little Bird Says, 'No!'" (pages 45–52)

- Picture Cards (pages 67–71)

- Heavy paper or cardstock

- Markers or crayons

- Scissors or paper cutter

- Laminating film (optional)

- Resealable plastic bags

## What to Do:

Before this activity, prepare the Picture Cards (page 67–71). Note that each series of cards presents a scenario and gives children an opportunity to decide what they should do if they are faced with that situation. This procedure will help them become aware of their ability to make good choices when having to make decisions about drugs. Reproduce and color each set of cards. You may wish to laminate the cards before cutting them apart. Store each set in separate resealable plastic bags. You may wish to make copies of each set for every child in your classroom. Then parents can use the cards to help their children practice the same skills at home.

Begin this activity by reading the story, "Little Bird Says, 'No!'" Talk with children about the characters in the story and the situations that Little Bird must face. Then use the Picture Cards to describe specific scenarios with children. Encourage them to discuss what they would do in each situation. Repeat this activity many times to help young children process the information.

## What to Say:

First I am going to read you a story about Little Bird. Listen carefully so you will know if she is able to make good choices when someone offers drugs to her. *(Read aloud the story.)* Let's talk about what Little Bird did to keep herself safe from people who wanted her to use drugs. *(Lead a discussion about the story.)* Now I am going to show you some picture cards that tell stories. After I show you each set of cards, you will get to tell the class what you would do next. *(Show the first set of cards.)* What is happening in this set of cards? *(Invite children to describe the events shown in the cards.)* What should you do next? *(Encourage children to discuss possible responses to the scenario shown in the cards.)*

# What Should You Do? *(cont.)*

# What Should You Do? *(cont.)*

# What Should You Do? *(cont.)*

| 1 | 2 |
|---|---|
| 3 | 4 |

# What Should You Do? *(cont.)*

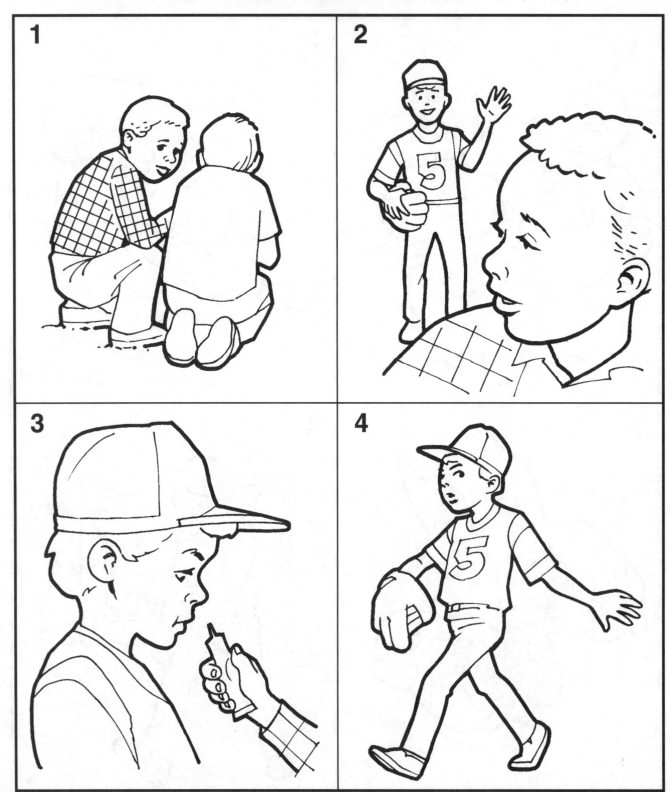

# What Should You Do? *(cont.)*

# Death and Grief

## Section Introduction

Coping with Death and Grief (page 73)

## Story

"Andrew and His Goldfish" (pages 74–84)

This story shows how a little boy goes through the grieving process after the death of his beloved goldfish. His mother provides important support for his emotional needs.

## Stick Puppet and Flannelboard Patterns

These patterns (pages 85–88) can be used to help children understand the issues that are emphasized in the story.

## Activities

- The Death of a Pet (pages 89 and 90)

- Pet Memorial (pages 91 and 92)

- A Poem About Sadness (pages 93 and 94)

- Different Ways People Show Sadness (pages 95–100)

- Flower Faces (page 101)

- Sympathy Cards (pages 102–104)

All of these activities help children realize that death is a natural part of life and that it is a normal part of the healing process to grieve for family members, friends, and pets that have died.

# Coping with Death and Grief

## The Subject of Death

Death is a difficult problem for children, as well as many adults, to face. It is important for children to learn how to deal with the grief they feel after losing someone or something they love. When discussing death and grief, it is important to consider the following.

1. Your tone of voice is just as important as the words you say.
2. Children need to understand and accept the reality of death to the best of their abilities.
3. The topic of death should not be ignored just because it is difficult to discuss.
4. Provide time for children to tell how they feel or to ask questions about their concerns regarding death. Listen carefully to their questions and comments because these will reveal any misconceptions and fears they may have.
5. Grief can be expressed in a variety of ways including anger, sadness, depression, and guilt. Anyone dealing with death should be allowed to express his/her feelings. There is no time limit put on how long someone should grieve. Some people will grieve longer than others.
6. Give simple facts to explain what death is. Children will be confused by long or complex explanations.
7. Point out that death is a natural part of life. Explain that all living things must eventually die.
8. Children do not suddenly become adults just because a parent has died. They must be allowed to continue being children.
9. You may wish to have the school counselor talk to particular children who seem to be having an especially difficult time dealing with death.
10. Do not be afraid to let children know that you do not know the answers to all their questions.
11. Use appropriate touch, such as hugs, holding hands, or pats on the back, to give children reassurance.
12. Never tell children how they should or should not feel about death.
13. You may wish to tell children about your own experiences to help them realize that everyone must deal with death.
14. Provide comfort to any child who is grieving. Help children try to remember the happy times that they spent with the loved ones they have lost.

## In This Book

This book provides a variety of suggestions to help children deal with death. The section begins with a story about a boy whose goldfish dies (pages 74–84), giving children a better understanding of death and the need to grieve. Stick puppet and flannel board patterns (pages 85–88) are provided for children to role-play the story as well as their own experiences, fears, and concerns. Activities (pages 89–104) are included to help children understand and cope with death.

# Andrew and His Goldfish

"Mommy," said Andrew. "Something is wrong with Goldie. She is floating upside down in her bowl."

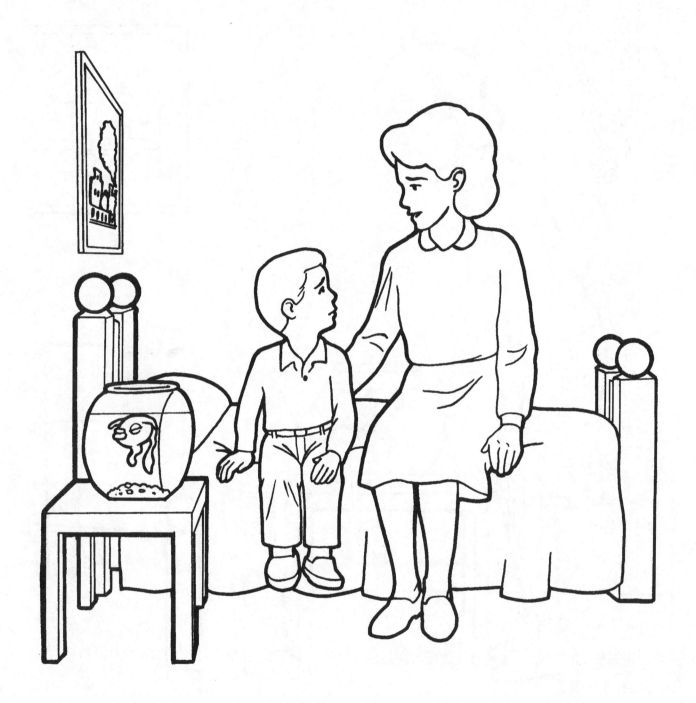

"I'm sorry, Andrew," said Mommy. "Goldie is dead. Goldfish have very short lives."

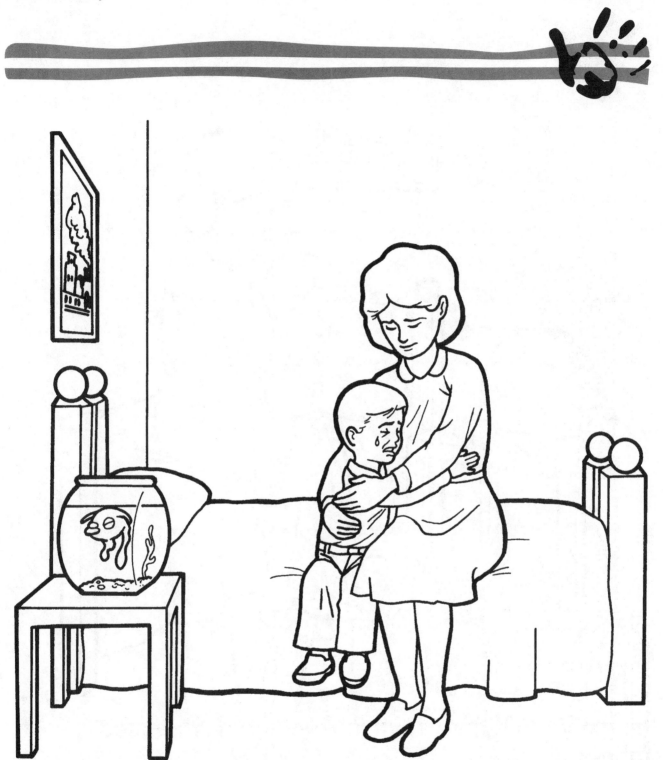

Andrew cried, "But she was my friend. I don't want her to be dead."

"I know sweetheart, but dying is a natural part of life," said Mommy. "It's very sad to lose a friend." Mommy held Andrew close while he cried.

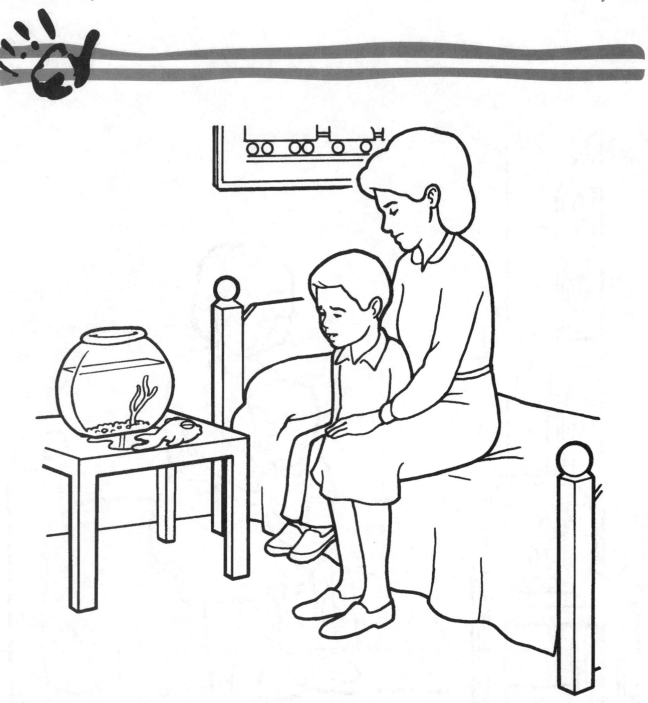

"Mommy, isn't there anything we can do?" sniffed Andrew.

Mommy looked thoughtfully at Andrew. "When a person dies, we have a funeral or a memorial. That is one way we can all be together and talk about how much we loved that person and tell why he or she was special. Would you like to do the same thing for Goldie?"

"How can we do that, Mommy?" Andrew wondered.

"First let's pick a pretty place in our garden to bury Goldie. Then we will find a small cardboard box and put her in it. After we bury her, we can tell why she was special to us."

"I think I would like to sing a song," said Andrew.

"That's a lovely idea," said Mommy.

Andrew and Mommy went outside to the garden. It was a beautiful place with pretty green grass, colorful flowers, and butterflies all around.

"Goldie would have thought this was pretty," said Andrew quietly.

"Then it's the perfect spot," said Mommy.

Mommy and Andrew went back inside. While Mommy got a small cardboard box and lined it with soft tissue paper, Andrew made a grave marker by decorating a popsicle stick with Goldie's name.

Mommy carefully lifted Goldie into the box, and Andrew gently covered it with the lid. Then they took the box and the grave marker to the garden. Together they dug a small hole for Goldie's grave.

"What shall we say, Mommy?" asked Andrew.

"Let's talk about why we loved Goldie," said Mommy. "I loved Goldie because she was fun to watch."

"I loved her because she was my friend. I could talk to her every day. I liked feeding her and cleaning her bowl," said Andrew.

"Now I will sing," said Andrew. Andrew sang his favorite song for Goldie. After he had finished singing the song, Andrew and Mommy placed the little box in the grave and covered it with dirt.

Andrew stuck the grave marker in the ground.

Then Mommy and Andrew hugged each other.

"How long will I feel sad?" sighed Andrew.

"I don't know," answered Mommy. "But one day you will think about Goldie and all the happy memories you have of her. Then you will feel better, and you will know that she lives in your heart forever."

# Stick Puppet and Flannelboard Patterns

### Andrew

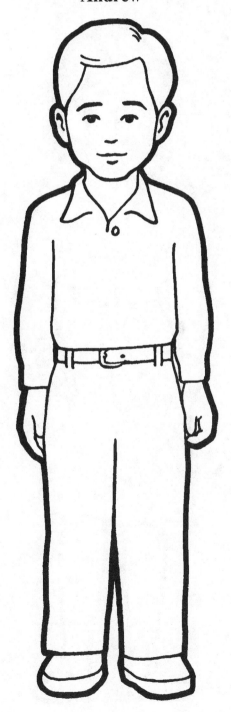

# Stick Puppet and Flannelboard Patterns *(cont.)*

## Andrew's Mommy

# Stick Puppet and Flannelboard Patterns *(cont.)*

**Goldie**

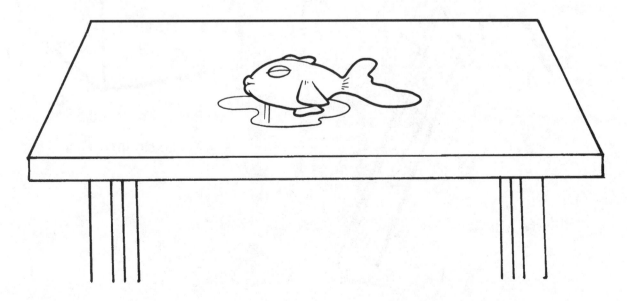

# Stick Puppet and Flannelboard
# Patterns *(cont.)*

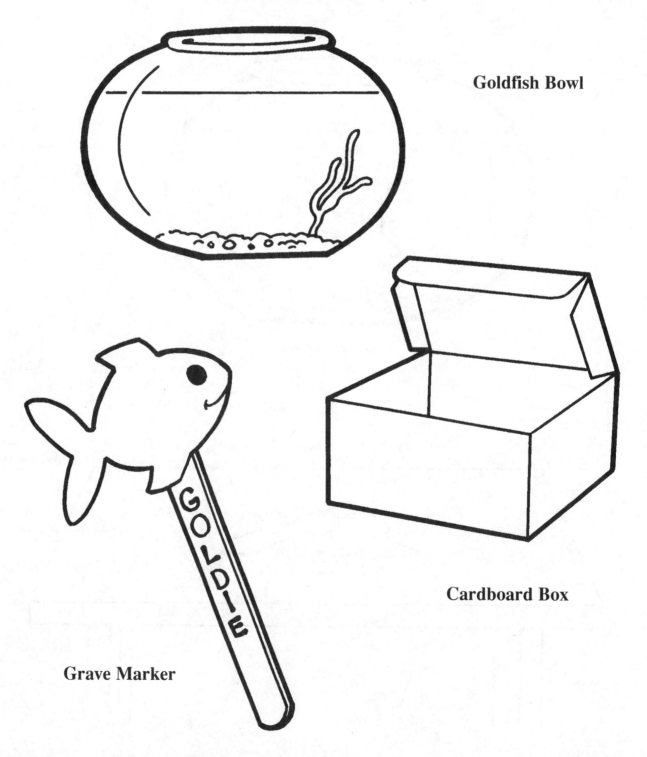

**Goldfish Bowl**

**Cardboard Box**

**Grave Marker**

# The Death of a Pet

## Purpose:

The purpose of this activity is to give young children an opportunity to start and direct their own grieving process, by thinking about, stating, and celebrating the 10 best things about the person, pet, or thing they lost.

## Preparation Time: One hour

## What You Need:

- *The Tenth Good Thing About Barney* by Judith Viorst (See page 10.)
- "Andrew and His Goldfish" (pages 74–84)
- The Ten Best Things About My Pet (page 90), one copy per child
- Pencils
- Drawing paper
- Markers, crayons, and other art supplies

## What to Do:

In this activity, children will have the opportunity to think about pets that have died and tell ten things that made the pets special to them. If some children have never had pets, have them talk about a special toy that was lost or broken.

Before beginning this activity, reproduce page 90 for children. First read aloud *The Tenth Good Thing About Barney* by Judith Viorst and/or "Andrew and His Goldfish." Both stories can be used to help children better understand death and the feelings of grief that accompany the death of a pet. After reading one or both stories, encourage children to tell the ten best things about their dead pets, real or imaginary. Help them write their ideas on the copies of page 90. Ask students to draw pictures of their pets on the drawing paper. Then, during circle time, invite children to share their lists and pictures with the class. You may wish to combine this activity with the Pet Memorial (pages 91 and 92).

**Note:** While this activity is geared toward the death of pets, there are certainly going to be plenty of instances in children's lives when they are grieving the death of people. This method, while simple, is an excellent way to help children begin their grieving process.

## What to Say:

I am going to read a story about a child who has a pet that dies. *(Read aloud and discuss* The Tenth Good Thing About Barney *and/or* "Andrew and His Goldfish.") Pets can be very good friends to us, and it makes us feel sad when they die. Have you ever had a pet that has died? *(Allow children to share their personal experiences with death. It is important to maintain an environment in which children feel safe talking about those they love who have died.)* Now we are going to draw pictures and write ten things about our pets that made them special to us.

# The Ten Best Things About My Pet

♥ _____

_____

♥ _____

_____

♥ _____

_____

♥ _____

_____

_____

♥ _____

_____

♥ _____

_____

♥ _____

_____

♥ _____

_____

♥ _____

_____

♥ _____

_____

# Pet Memorial

## Purpose:
A memorial is for the living and attempts to bring closure to the life of a beloved person or pet. In this activity, children will create memorial wreaths for pets that have died.

## Preparation Time: Several afternoons

## What You Need:
- Heart Wreath (page 92)
- The Death of a Pet (pages 89 and 90, optional)

## What to Do:
Before this activity, gather the materials listed to make the heart wreaths. You may wish to enlist the help of parent volunteers or older students for this part of the activity. Show children how to make a wreath using the directions on page 92. Then invite them to make their own wreaths. Provide assistance as needed. **Warning:** Be sure an adult handles the rubber cement.

You may wish to combine this activity with the one on pages 89 and 90.

## Heart Wreath Alternatives:
- Instead of using wrapping paper to cover the hearts, you may wish to provide a variety of wallpaper samples.

- As a second alternative, you can have students make cushion-type heart shapes out of double wrapping paper or wallpaper scraps that are stuffed with tissue paper and then stapled around the edges.

**Note:** While this activity is geared toward the death of pets, there are certainly going to be plenty of instances in children's lives when they are grieving the death of people. This method, while simple, is an excellent way to help children begin their grieving process.

## What to Say:
When people die, we often have something called a memorial. This is a time when friends and family gather around and remember the person. You often see wreaths of flowers at memorials. We can have the same kind of ceremony for our pets that have died. It is important to grieve when someone or something you love has died. Grieving is when you feel sad and miss that person or pet very much. Today we are going to make heart wreaths for our memorials. You may wish to write your pet's name on your wreath. *(Help children make the wreaths.)* Let's hang up our wreaths and you can tell us something special about your pet. *(You may wish to allow children to use their lists from page 90 for this part of the activity.)*

# Heart Wreath

## Materials:

- Paper plates, one per child
- Tagboard
- Safety scissors, one pair per child
- Assorted wrapping paper scraps
- Pencils
- Glue sticks
- Rubber cement, for adult use only

## Directions:

1. Cut the center out of the paper plates. Cut out heart shapes from the tagboard. Trace the tagboard heart shapes onto the wrapping paper and cut out them out.
2. Glue the wrapping paper to the tagboard hearts with a glue stick.
3. Glue the hearts to the paper plates with rubber cement.

# A Poem About Sadness

## Purpose:

Just as many adults find solace in music or poetry during times of sadness, children can also benefit from these things. The purpose of this activity is to give children outlets for their feelings of grief.

## Preparation Time: One hour

## What You Need:

- "It's Okay to Feel Sad" (page 94), one copy per child
- Crayons
- Chart tablet (optional)
- Tape recorder (optional)
- Cassette tape of soft music (optional)

## What to Do:

In this activity, you will share a poem about sadness with children and let them have the opportunity to read and color their own copies of the poem. This simple poem about sadness puts the feeling of grief into simple, easy-to-understand language. Children will find comfort in the poem. It will help them realize that death is a natural part of life and that it is normal to have feelings of grief when people or pets die.

Prior to doing this activity, reproduce the poem. You may wish to use a chart tablet to make an enlarged copy of the poem to hang up in the classroom. Then read the poem aloud to the children and discuss it with them. Ask volunteers to share experiences with death and sadness. Accept all responses. For example, some children may tell stories of feeling sad over a lost or broken toy. Point out to the class that grief can be felt any time something special is gone.

Encourage children to color their copies of the poem. While children are coloring, they may enjoy listening to some soft music. The music can help create a quiet and reflective mood for the activity. Then invite children to share the poems with their families.

## What to Say:

Today I am going to read aloud a poem entitled "It's Okay to Be Sad." This poem tells some of the reasons that people feel sad. It explains that everyone has times when they feel sad and that it is okay to feel this way. First I will read the poem to you, and then we will talk about it. *(Read aloud and discuss the poem.)* When have you felt sad? *(Invite volunteers to respond.)* What can you do to help a friend who feels sad? *(Encourage each child to respond.)* Now I will give you your own copy of the poem. You may color it and take it home to share with your family. *(Give each child a copy of the poem and provide crayons for children to use.)*

# It's Okay to Feel Sad

Sometimes we feel sad
And that is okay.
We feel sad for many reasons.
And in different ways.
Sometimes it's because
We have lost something dear —
The thing that we loved
Is no longer here.

It's okay to feel sad
When this happens to you.
It's okay to cry.
And to feel blue.
It's okay to need hugs.
And to talk to a friend.
Then you will feel better,
And the hurting will end.

Hearts can get scrapes
And bruised sometimes too,
Hurting from the loss,
Will heal inside you.
The sadness you feel
Will one day go away,
And then you will know
That you are okay.

When you see a sad friend,
Don't just say to smile.
Sit down with your friend —
Hold hands for awhile.
One day all the sadness
Will drift far away,
And the friend that you helped
Will soon feel okay.

# Different Ways People Show Sadness

## Purpose:

The purpose of this activity is to give children an understanding of the various ways people express feelings of sadness. This activity also helps them begin to become sensitive to the feelings of others.

## Preparation Time: One afternoon

## What You Need:

- Emotion Pictures (pages 96–100)
- Markers or crayons
- Plastic page protectors with three holes
- Three-ring binder

## What to Do:

Before presenting this activity, prepare an Emotion Book using the following directions. Reproduce the Emotion Pictures. Use markers or crayons to color them. Insert the pictures into plastic page protectors. Then place the pages into the three-ring binder. When you talk to children about the activity, you will have a flip-picture-book to show them.

Begin this activity by talking with children about feeling sad. Then mention that not everyone shows sadness in the same way. Use the Emotion Book to show pictures of children expressing their sadness in different ways. Point out that the reason someone behaves a certain way may be difficult to understand.

The following pictures are presented in the Emotion Book:

- A sad child who is laughing and cracking jokes to feel better
- A sad child who is angry
- A sad child who is withdrawn
- A sad child who is crying
- A sad child who is afraid

## What to Say:

Sometimes when we feel sad, we might cry. Have you ever cried when you felt sad? Have you ever been angry when you felt sad? Have you ever been afraid when you felt sad? What did you do? Let's look at some pictures to see what these children are doing. Here is a child who is smiling and laughing. How could he be sad? (*Let students respond.*) That's right. He might be trying to make himself feel better.

# Emotion Pictures

# Emotion Pictures *(cont.)*

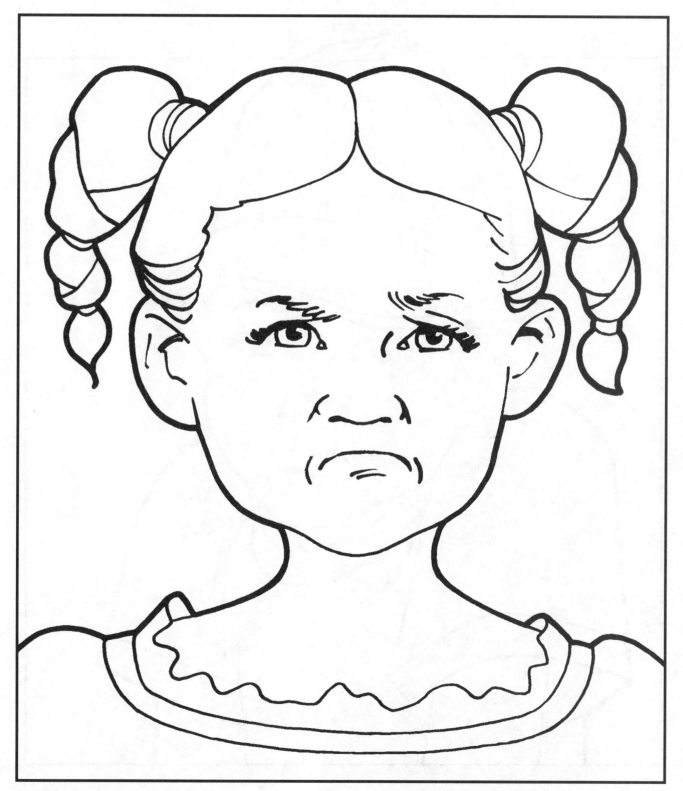

# Emotion Pictures *(cont.)*

# Emotion Pictures *(cont.)*

# Emotion Pictures *(cont.)*

# Flower Faces

## Purpose:

This activity is an extension of the one on pages 95–100. It allows children to use paper plate faces to show the different emotions people have during times of grief.

**Preparation Time:** A few minutes

## What You Need:

- Paper plates, several per child

- Construction paper

- Safety scissors, one pair per child

- Non-toxic glue

- Markers or crayons

- Pie tins or other sturdy containers, one for every two or three children

- Craft sticks, one per child

## What to Do:

Fold construction paper into squares and cut out circles. You may wish to let children experiment with cutting their own circle shapes using the construction paper and safety scissors. Explain that the circles are the flower petals. They will be easy for children to handle and glue. Provide small amounts of glue in pie tins or other sturdy containers. Two or three children should be able to share a container of glue. Have children use craft sticks to spread the glue.

Demonstrate for the class how to glue the flower petals onto the rim of a paper plate. Ask children to do the same on their plates. Then show how to draw a happy face in the center of the flower. Allow children to do the same.

Discuss the different emotions that people feel when they are grieving over the loss of a pet or a person they loved. Encourage children to make additional flower faces that show these different emotions.

## What to Say:

Think about the Emotion Pictures we have already looked at. *(You may wish to review the pictures on pages 96–100.)* What kinds of feelings did they show? *(Have children respond.)* Today we are going to make Flower Faces. Like the Emotion Pictures, these faces will show how you may feel after the death of a pet or person you love. First we will make the flowers. This is what they will look like. *(Show children a sample flower without the face drawn on it. Then have them make their flowers.)* Now we will draw faces on our flowers. Make each face that you draw show a different feeling that you may have when a pet or person you love has died.

# Sympathy Cards

## Purpose:

The purpose of this activity is to give children an opportunity to help someone else who is grieving. Children make and give sympathy cards to friends or family members who are grieving.

## Preparation: One hour

## What You Need:

- Sympathy Cards (pages 103 and 104)
- Scissors or paper cutter
- Glue
- Watercolor paints (optional)
- Envelopes
- Heavy paper or cardstock
- Markers and crayons
- Glitter
- Paintbrushes (optional)

## What to Do:

Before this activity, set up a card-making center in your classroom that children can use as they wish. In the center, provide art supplies, glue, construction paper, and copies of the Sympathy Cards (pages 103 and 104).

**Note:** While this particular activity is for making sympathy cards, it is possible to make a center in which children can make a variety of cards using different themes.

Before presenting this activity, reproduce the Sympathy Cards on heavy paper or cardstock. Then cut out and decorate several samples to show the children. After telling children about the activity and showing them the samples, place your cards in the center for them to examine. You may wish to simulate sending the cards rather than actually sending them.

## Alternative:

Another idea is to make this activity a class project in order to send a sympathy card to a classmate whose family has suffered a loss. To do this, make a large card that every child can sign. Assist children who cannot write their own names by lightly writing the names on the card and asking them to trace over their names.

## What to Say:

When people feel sad, it is important to let them know that someone cares about them. One way you can show someone who is grieving over the death of a pet or person that you care about is to send a sympathy card. We are all going to have a chance to make sympathy cards to show the people we love that we care about them. Here are some sample cards that I have made. *(Show the sample cards.)* Now you will get to use the card-making center to decorate your own cards.

# Sympathy Cards *(cont.)*

Sometimes when we are feeling sad

it's nice to know we have a friend.

I am thinking of you,

and I hope you feel happier soon.

Gray skies don't last forever, but my love for you will.

Deepest Sympathy

# Sympathy Cards *(cont.)*

Some things in life make us sad
and it is okay to cry.

We might feel unhappy
for awhile.

But one day soon
we will smile again.

I just wanted you to know
that I am thinking about you.

---

I love you very much.
and I am sorry you are sad.

Here are some things to
think about that might help
to cheer you up:
rainbows, ice cream,
kittens, puppies,
flowers, sunshine,
hugs, kisses
and smiles.

Most of all, don't forget
I love you.

# Tolerance

## Section Introduction

Teaching Tolerance (page 106)

## Story

"Families" (pages 107–118)

A story that describes many different kinds of families. It shows that families have similarities and differences.

## Stick Puppet and Flannelboard Patterns

These patterns (pages 119–125) can be used to help children understand the issues that are emphasized in the story.

## Activities

- My Family Picture Book (page 126)
- Celebrate Our Differences (page 127)
- Senior Pen Pals (pages 128–130)
- Homeless Shelter Donation Drive (pages 131–133)
- Chain of Children (pages 134 and 135)

All of these activities focus on potential bias and help to reinforce tolerant behavior. The issues of ethnic background, gender, age, socio-economic status, and personal preferences are addressed.

# Teaching Tolerance

## Learning to Get Along

Tolerance is a learned behavior. Therefore, it is important for children to be shown tolerant behavior in their homes, schools, and communities. Children must recognize that there are many different types of peoples and ways of living. They should learn that it is important not to judge others or discriminate against them. Children must try to understand and learn to celebrate the things that make them similar to, as well as different from, their classmates. They must respect the various backgrounds, beliefs, customs, and personal preferences of other people. This will help them realize that their friends, classmates, and neighbors do not need to be exactly like them.

## Why Teach Tolerance?

Teaching tolerance is important for the following reasons:

1. Children are better prepared to live harmoniously in a multiethnic society.
2. Children recognize the importance of cooperation among different people.
3. Children realize that all people have the same basic needs, such as food, clothing, and shelter.
4. Children notice that all people participate in many of the same types of activities, such as going to school, listening to music, reading stories, and creating things using arts and crafts.
5. Children learn to have positive self-images by having opportunities to share information about themselves.

## Ways to Promote the Acceptance of Others

1. Read aloud the poem "Children, Children Everywhere" by Jack Prelutsky. Have children draw pictures to go with the poem.
2. Play a variety of folk music for children.
3. Read aloud folk tales from different countries.
4. Have children brainstorm a list of the ways in which all children are the same. Write the list on the chalkboard.
5. Have children learn to sing "It's a Small World" by Richard M. Sherman and Robert B. Sherman.

## In This Book

This book provides a variety of suggestions to help children learn tolerance by exploring the similarities and differences among peoples. The section begins with a story about tolerance (pages 107-118), showing children that there are many different kinds of families and all of them are important. Stick puppet and flannel board patterns (pages 119–125) are provided for children to role-play the story as well as their own experiences. Activities (pages 126–135) are included that create an atmosphere of understanding and acceptance in the classroom. These activities will help children understand and learn tolerance.

# Families

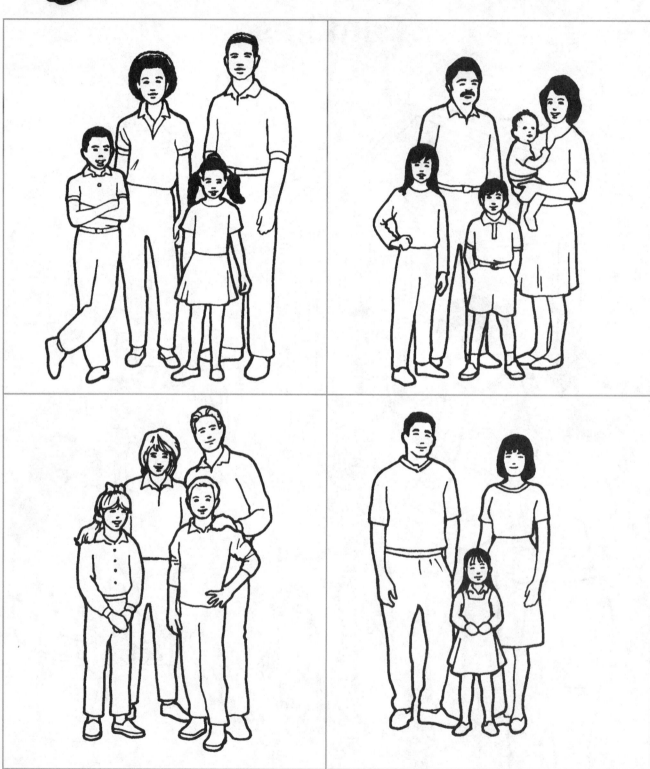

Most people have families, but not all families are the same.

Some families have a mommy and a daddy and some children.

Some families have only one parent with children. The parent can be the mommy or the daddy.

Some mommies and daddies get divorced and don't live together anymore. When this happens, some children live with only one parent. Other children live with their mommies some of the time and with their daddies some of the time.

Sometimes divorced mommies and daddies marry other people. Then the children might have new brothers and sisters called stepbrothers and stepsisters.

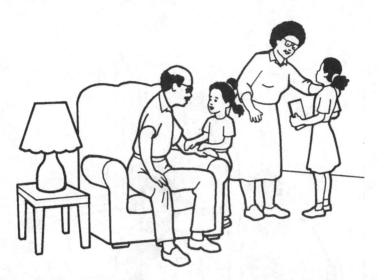

Some families have children who live with their grandmas and grandpas instead of their mommies and daddies. Grandparents love and care for the children just like other parents.

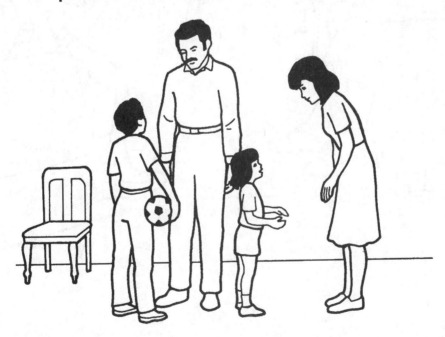

Some children live with their aunts and uncles instead of their mommies and daddies. They also love and care for the children like other parents.

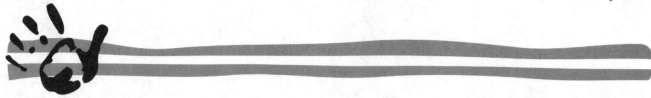

Some families are very large. Relatives, such as grandmas, grandpas, aunts, and uncles, may live with the mommies, daddies, and children.

Some children live with foster parents. Foster parents care for the children because the real mommies and daddies cannot.

Some children are adopted. There are many reasons why parents choose to adopt their children. Mommies and daddies who adopt love and care for the children just like other parents.

Families are the same in many ways, but they are also different. This doesn't mean that one family is better than another.

Your family may not be like anyone else's, but it is special and important to you.

Draw a picture of your family on this page.

# Stick Puppet and Flannelboard Patterns

**Daddies**

# Stick Puppet and Flannelboard Patterns *(cont.)*

**Mommies**

# Stick Puppet and Flannelboard Patterns *(cont.)*

## Children

# Stick Puppet and Flannelboard Patterns *(cont.)*

**Grandmas**

# Stick Puppet and Flannelboard Patterns *(cont.)*

### Grandpas

# Stick Puppet and Flannelboard Patterns *(cont.)*

## Aunts

# Stick Puppet and Flannelboard Patterns *(cont.)*

**Uncles**

# My Family Picture Book

## Purpose:

This activity helps children become aware of their families. Then they can compare/contrast their families with other children's families.

## Preparation Time: Two hours

## What You Need:

- White paper
- Three-ring binder (notebook)
- Three-hole punch (or three-holed paper without lines available at drug or stationary stores)
- Crayons
- Markers
- Glitter glue
- Photographs of family members (optional)

## What to Do:

Provide binders or ask parents to send binders with their children. Allow children to individualize the covers of the binders by decorating them and writing their names using glitter glue. Then provide children with white paper. You may wish to invite parents to send family photographs that can be used for this activity. Be sure to let parents know that these pictures will be glued to paper for their children's family picture books. Have children create drawings of different family members on the paper. Children who do not have photographs can draw family members from memory. Punch holes in each page, and help them place their drawings and photographs in the binders. Write the names of the family members below each drawing.

Most children will enjoy drawing family members they see every day. However, many will have other relatives, such as grandparents, uncles, aunts, and cousins, that they do not see very often. You may wish to ask parents to send labeled photographs of these relatives, too. Then the children will have the opportunity to share their photographs, and you can explain who these relatives are. Encourage children to add the photographs and their drawings of these relatives to their binders. After the binders are completed, allow children time to share their pictures. Ask children to compare and contrast their families.

## What to Say:

Today you are going to make a family picture book. You will use a binder, or notebook, and paper. To make your book, you are going to decorate the binder cover and draw pictures of the people in your family to put inside of it. Then I will help you write the names of those people below the pictures that you draw. When all of the books are finished, you will show yours to the class and tell us about your family. Then we will talk about how your family is the same or different from other families.

# Celebrate Our Differences

## Purpose:

This activity will help children realize that the world is populated by different kinds of people. Children will gain an understanding of and appreciation for ethnic and individual differences.

## Preparation Time: One afternoon

## What You Need:

- Magazines and newspapers
- Scissors
- Double-sided tape
- Hand mirrors, one for each child or pair of children

## What to Do:

Ahead of time, prepare a bulletin board and gather magazines and newspapers that can be used to cut out pictures of people's faces. Distribute the hand mirrors to children. Pairs of children may need to share the mirrors depending on the number that you have available. To begin this activity, have children look at themselves in the mirrors. Ask them to describe themselves. Then have children compare and contrast their appearances.

Have children cut out the magazine and newspaper pictures of people's faces. Provide help as needed. Ask them to make a collection of pictures that show different kinds of faces. Point out to the children how people have different appearances.

Place double-sided tape on the back of each picture. Allow a few children at a time to place the pictures on the bulletin board, making a collage of faces. Encourage them to discuss the different features that the faces have. You may wish to let them change the pictures on a regular basis.

## What to Say:

You may have noticed that there are many different kinds of people in our school and in our neighborhood. This is true in schools and neighborhoods all over the world. One of the things that makes you special is that your face is different from anyone else's. I am going to give you a mirror. You need to hold it carefully so it won't break. *(Pass out the mirrors.)* Look at the color of your eyes. Do you think everyone in our class has the same eye color? *(Have children respond.)* Now let's see what eye colors you have. Raise your hand if you have blue eyes. Raise your hand if you have brown eyes. Raise your hand if you have green or hazel eyes. *(Each time have children respond.)* What other differences do you notice? *(Have children respond.)*

Now, let's look at the magazines and newspapers. Find pictures of people's faces. When you find some faces you like, cut them out. Then I will help you tape them onto the bulletin board. After the collage is done, we will talk about how the faces are different.

# Senior Pen Pals

## Purpose:

The purpose of this activity is to help children learn to respect and appreciate older people.

## Preparation Time: Several days

## What You Need:

- Pen Pal Letter (page 129)
- Senior Organization Letter (page 130)
- Art supplies
- Camera and film (optional)

## What to Do:

In this activity, children have the opportunity to interact with senior citizens, as a class and/or as individuals. Invite the residents of a senior center in your community to make valuable contributions to your children by becoming adopted "grandparents." There are many seniors who either do not have any grandchildren or are not able to see their grandchildren on a regular basis. Getting together with a senior organization is an ideal way for children to interact with "grandparents" who are likely to enjoy giving the youngsters positive feedback and nurturing.

Begin this activity by selecting and contacting a local senior organization. A letter (page 130) has been provided for you to use for this purpose. If the response is negative, try contacting a different center. Otherwise, talk to the director about setting up the pen-pal activity. You may wish to host an in-school party for the participating seniors to meet the children, or it may be easier for you to take the children to the center. Take photographs of this event if at all possible. Even if an actual visit is not possible, children will enjoy keeping in contact with their adopted "grandparents" via the mail or e-mail.

Discuss with children what a pen pal is. To start the process, have children use the Pen Pal Letter (page 129) for their first letters. Throughout the year, have children respond to the letters they receive by dictating letters for you to write, drawing pictures, or making small gifts for their pen pals. You will notice that this correspondence will be very meaningful to the children and senior citizens. If possible, take photographs of the children to send to their pen pals.

## What to Say:

We are very lucky because the people at _____ Center want to be our "adopted grandparents." Our "adopted grandparents" will be our pen pals. Pen pals are people who write back and forth to each other. Have you ever written to your grandma or grandpa before? Why did you write? *(Allow time for discussion.)* I will help you send your pen pal letters, stories, pictures, photographs, and small gifts that you make.

# Pen Pal Letter

Date _____

Dear _____ ,

```
┌─────────────────────────────────────────────────────────┐
│                                                           │
│                                                           │
│                                                           │
│                                                           │
│                                                           │
│                                                           │
│                                                           │
│                                                           │
└─────────────────────────────────────────────────────────┘
```

Hello.  My name is _____ . Here is a picture of me.

I am _____ years old.

I go to _____ School.

I like to _____ .

My favorite book is _____ .

My favorite TV show is _____ .

Another interesting fact about me is that I _____

_____ .


Your friend,

_____

# Senior Organization Letter

Date _____

Dear Senior Organization Director,

As part of a class unit, I am interested in having pen pals to give my students the opportunity to interact with senior citizens. Some children do not have any contact with their grandparents. Others have only limited contact. I am hoping the residents at your facility would be willing to be our "adopted grandparents." I feel that the children and the senior citizens would greatly benefit from being pen pals.

I will follow up with a phone call later this week to discuss the project in greater detail. Thank you for your time and consideration. I look forward to speaking with you.

Sincerely,

_____
Teacher

_____
School

_____
Telephone

# Homeless Shelter Donation Drive

## Purpose:
The purpose of this activity is to teach children about some of the problems that homeless people face and help them develop empathy for those people who are in need. It encourages children to help others.

**Preparation Time:** Ongoing over several weeks or months

## What You Need:
- Donation request letter (page 132)
- Letter to shelter (page 133)
- Cardboard boxes
- Place to store donations
- Vehicle to transport donations
- Camera and film

## What to Do:
Prepare for this activity by selecting a local shelter for the homeless for which children can gather donations. Then contact this shelter using the letter on page 133.

Begin by discussing homelessness. It is important for children to understand that homelessness is something that happens to all different kinds of people. Children often have the misconception that a poor person is someone who is "bad" or "lazy." Explain that people become homeless for a variety of reasons. Possible reasons for homelessness include loss of employment/income; loss of savings/investments; loss of home due to foreclosure, a natural disaster, or an accident such as a fire. Point out that homeless people often seek help from community shelters. Explain that your class is going to help collect canned foods and other supplies to donate to a local shelter.

Send the donation request letter (page 132) to parents. After the donations have been collected, take a photograph of the children with their donations. This can be placed on a bulletin board to remind students about their helpfulness. Make an after-school delivery to the shelter and tell the class about it the next day. It is usually not a good idea to take children to a homeless shelter since one of them may be staying there and this could embarrass him or her.

## What to Say:
Have you ever seen someone you thought probably didn't have a home? What made you think that person was homeless? People who are homeless need help from others. Sometimes they go to a place called a shelter to get the help they need. Since it is important for people to help each other, our class is going to collect things that are needed by people who are at a local shelter. After we have gathered as many items as possible, I am going to drop these things off at the shelter. The next day, I will tell you all about my visit to the shelter.

# Donation Request Letter

Date _____

Dear Parent(s),

Our class is collecting canned goods and other items to donate to a local homeless shelter as part of a unit about helping others. We will be collecting these goods from _____ until _____ . Then I will deliver them. I believe this activity will help the children become more sensitive to the needs of others and teach them about the importance and joy of giving.

The shelter I have contacted is in need of the following items:

- •
- •
- •
- •
- •
- •
- •

If you can donate any of these items, please bring them to our classroom before or after school. If you have any questions, please feel free to call. Thank you for helping to make your child's school experience a positive one.

Sincerely,

_____
Teacher

_____
School

_____
Telephone

# Shelter Letter

Date _____

Dear Shelter Coordinator,

As part of a class project, we would like to make donations to a local homeless shelter. We are interested in helping your organization. Please let us know what kinds of donations you need or if any of the items listed below would be useful to your organization. All used items will be checked to ensure that they are in good condition.

We are probably able to obtain items such as:

- clothes
- toys
- canned goods
- small equipment
- books and magazines

Please feel free to contact me with any questions or concerns. The best time of day to reach me is at _____.

Sincerely,

_____

Teacher

_____

School

_____

Telephone

# Chain of Children

## Purpose:

This activity acquaints children with types of clothing worn by people from a variety of cultures. Children make a chain of paper dolls that are holding hands to represent the importance of cooperation among all peoples.

**Preparation Time:** Several afternoons

## What You Need:

- Paper Doll Patterns (page 135), one for each child
- Construction paper
- Art supplies
- Glue
- Scissors
- Fabric scraps
- Encyclopedias and nonfiction books about traditional clothing used in different cultures

## What to Do:

In this art activity, children learn about the types of traditional clothing that people wear in different cultures and use this information to decorate paper dolls. Then the paper dolls are displayed as a chain around a bulletin board or along a wall in the classroom.

Before this activity, spend an afternoon in your school or public library or on the Internet to find pictures of traditional clothing worn by people in other cultures. Then reproduce the Paper Doll Pattern on page 135. Use copies of the doll patterns and fabric scraps, construction paper, and other art supplies to create samples for children to examine.

Begin this activity by setting up an Art Center in your classroom. Then model how to make clothes for the paper dolls. Place your samples in the center. Provide encyclopedias and nonfiction books for children to look at pictures of different types of traditional clothing. Allow time for them to decorate their dolls. After children have completed their dolls, attach them to the bulletin board or along a wall, hand-to-hand in a line. Ask children why they think it is important to show the dolls holding hands.

## What to Say:

You are going to make paper dolls that show the traditional clothing that people wear in different parts of the world. Did you know that people in other places may not wear the same kinds of clothes you do? Let's look at some pictures of people from around the world. *(Show the pictures.)* Then we will make clothes for our paper dolls. When you are finished, I will hang up your paper dolls. I will put the dolls in a line so it looks like they are holding hands. Why do you think it is important to show the dolls holding hands? *(Solicit responses.)*

# Paper Doll Patterns

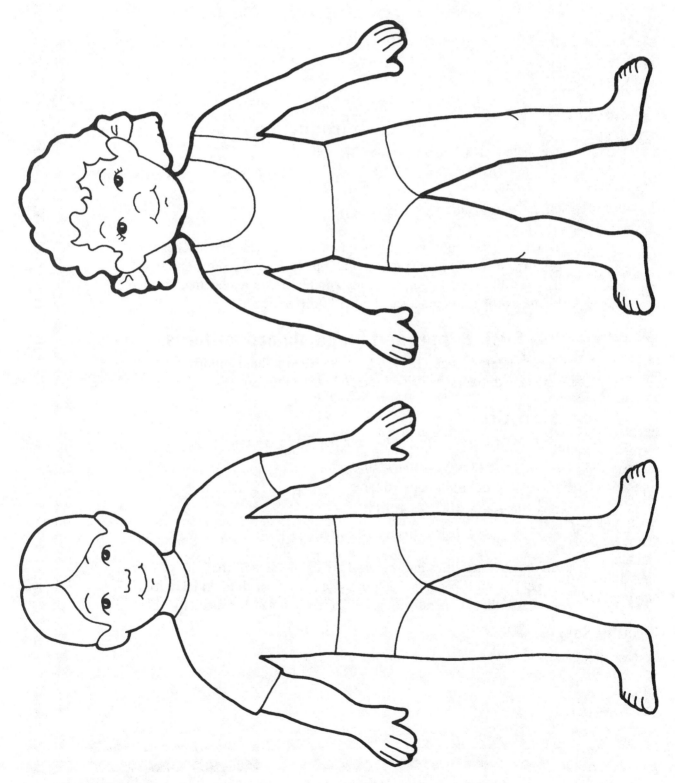

# Specially-Abled

## Section Introduction

Special Needs Children (pages 137)

## Story

"Benny's Wheels" (pages 138–150)

This is a story about Benny, a boy in a wheel chair, who teaches his best friend some of the ways in which people are the same and how they are different. Together Benny and his friend realize that "we are a rainbow of color and a salad bowl of differences."

## Stick Puppet and Flannelboard Patterns

These patterns (pages 151–154) can be used to help children understand the issues that are emphasized in the story.

## Activities

- Awareness of Special Needs (pages 155–160)
- Sit-Down Center (page 161)
- "Basket" Ball (page 162)
- Bean Bag Toss (page 163)
- Hearing Inpaired (pages 165–166)

All of these activities inform children about some of the issues faced by people with special needs. In these activities, children learn to work together cooperatively using games adapted for specially-abled students.

# Special Needs Children

## Creating an Environment of Acceptance

Children with disabilities are often placed in general, or regular, education classrooms with children of their own age. This placement allows them to develop a sense of community and fosters the social growth of all students.

Teachers must prepare the class to receive children with disabilities. They must be able to facilitate learning as well as promote the socialization necessary for specially-abled children to be valued members of the group. All children, disabled and nondisabled, should work together on cooperative learning projects and learning centers. They will attend school assemblies and extracurricular activities together. These interactions foster improved communication, greater cooperation, and a better understanding among class members.

Disabled children being included in a public school for the first time may experience a great deal of anxiety. The move can be a positive one if teachers and students at the new school are willing to learn and adapt. The children and classroom should be prepared ahead of time. Social adjustment is an important consideration because people who are well adjusted are free to learn.

Explain, as simply as possible, the diseases or handicaps that your included children have. You may also need to explain the difference between a disease and an injury. You may find it helpful to share some books about characters with similar conditions or problems to your special needs children. Discuss the characters' feelings and needs. Ask: *How are the characters like you? How do they communicate? What kinds of adaptations do handicapped students need to be successful?* As an alternative, you may prefer to show and discuss videos portraying disabled children in typical school settings.

Educators can create an environment of honesty and compassion. Teach children to respect the feelings of others. Support an anti-bias attitude by helping them understand that people have many similarities as well as differences.

Classrooms should be environments that foster cooperation and help children recognize their strengths and weaknesses. Be sure to give children a variety of opportunities to interact, share, and assist each other.

## In This Book

This book provides a variety of suggestions to help children deal with people who have special needs. The section begins with a story about a boy in a wheelchair who celebrates individual differences (pages 138–150). Stick puppet and flannel board patterns (pages 151-154) are provided for children to role-play the story as well as their own experiences with specially-abled people. The activities (pages 155–166) promote the idea of people, disabled and nondisabled, working cooperatively as a community.

# Benny's Wheels

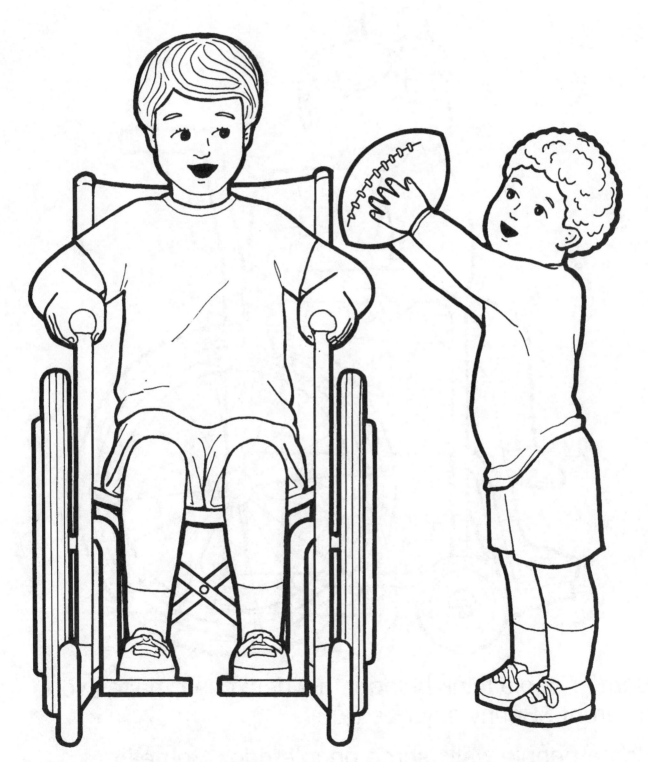

I have a friend named Benny. Benny has wheels.

Some people think being in a wheel chair makes you different.  Benny says it's true.

Some people walk; some people ride.  Sometimes Benny lets me ride too!

Benny says we all have things that make us different.

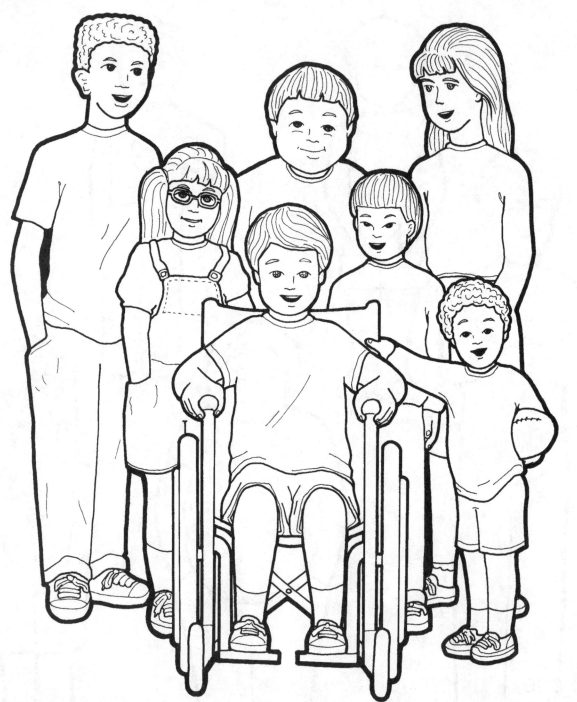

We look different. Some people are big, and some are small. Some are short, and some are tall. Some people have brown eyes. Other people have green eyes or blue eyes or hazel eyes.

We speak different languages. English, Spanish, Russian, Italian, Vietnamese, French, German, Polish, Japanese, Chinese, and Arabic are just some of the many languages.

There are many, many different ways to talk.

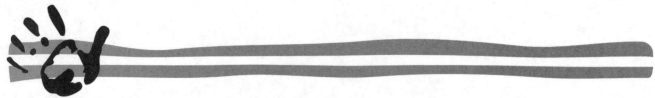

# Some people talk using their hands.

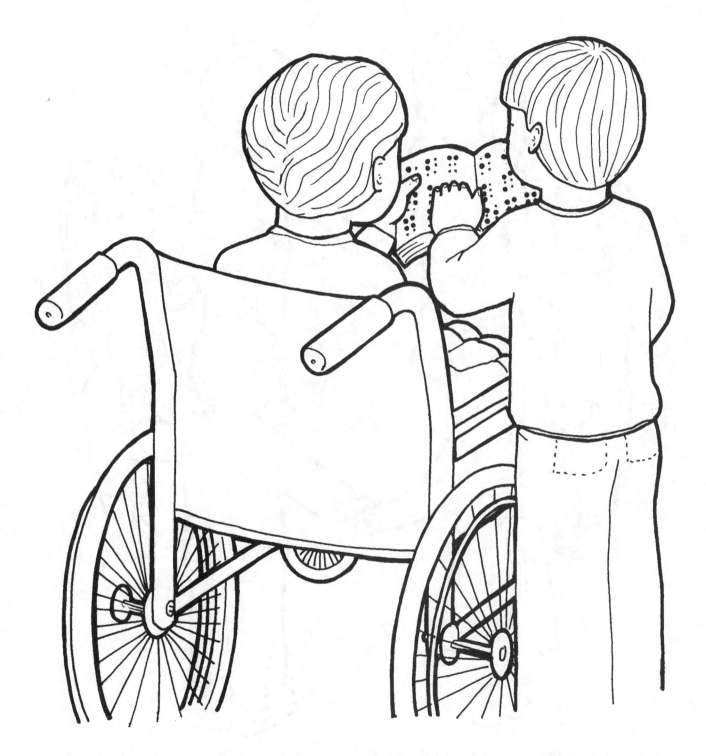

# Some people read Braille.

Benny says the important thing is that we find a way to talk to each other, no matter what it is.

Benny says, "We are a rainbow of colors and a salad bowl of differences."

Benny talks in pictures. When he says something, I can almost see it!

Benny says our differences make us special and that we are all special.

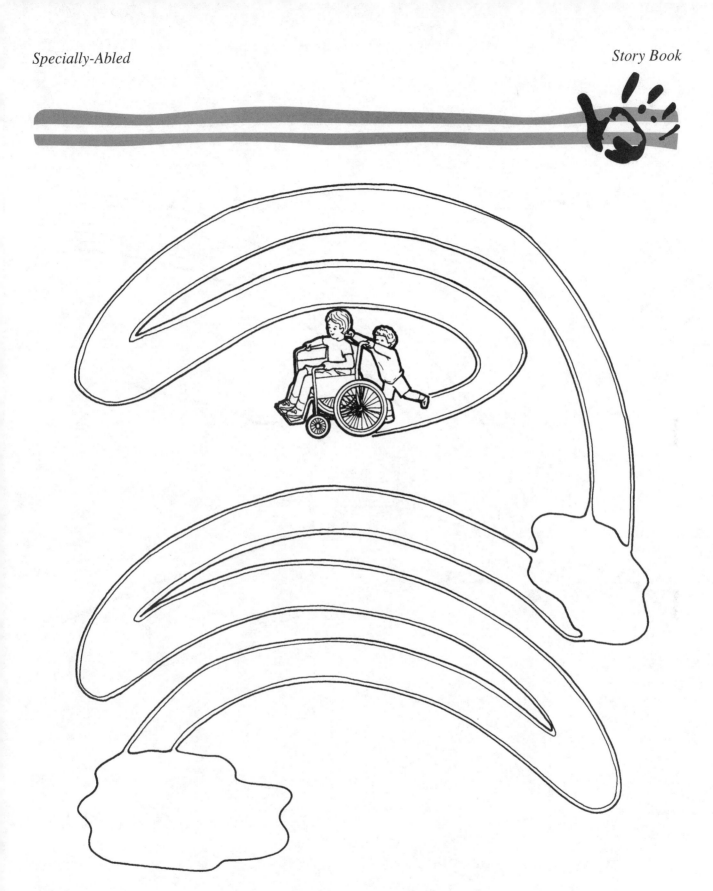

After it rains Benny and I make rainbows.

First we go through a puddle. Then we use the wheels on Benny's wheelchair to paint on the cement.

# Wouldn't you hate a world without rainbows?

# Stick Puppet and Flannelboard Patterns

**Benny**

# Stick Puppet and Flannelboard Patterns *(cont.)*

### Benny's Wheelchair

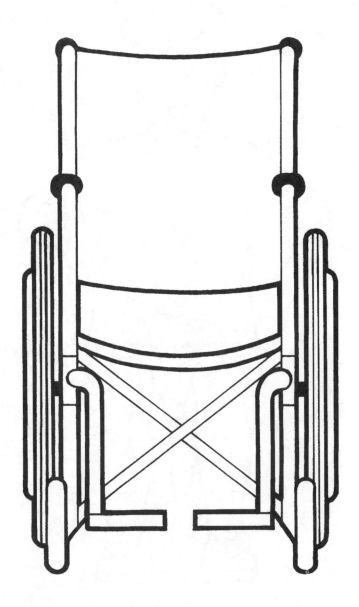

# Stick Puppet and Flannelboard Patterns *(cont.)*

## Benny's Best Friend

# Stick Puppet and Flannelboard Patterns *(cont.)*

## Neighborhood Kids

# Awareness of Special Needs

**Purpose:**

This activity allows children to increase their awareness of some accommodations and modifications that are made so handicapped students are able to function in school environments.

**Preparation Time:** One hour

**What You Need:**

- Pictures (pages 156–160)
- Crayons or markers

**What to Do:**

It is important for children to realize that some of their classmates may be specially-abled. They should be aware of how your school meets the needs of these students.

Children must be taught how to interact positively with children who have special needs. One of the first steps is show children your school is modified to make it easier for specially-abled students to attend.

Before beginning this activity, survey your school campus for any modifications that you can show children. If available, consider showing your class some or all of the following:

- ramps for children using wheelchairs, walkers, and crutches
- handicapped parking spaces
- curbs designed for wheelchair access
- adaptive bathroom facilities
- adaptive physical education equipment
- adaptive school bus
- adaptive furniture

Then, for the activity, take children on a walking tour of your campus to show them these things. Then show children the pictures (pages 156–160) and ask them which modifications they saw while on the walking tour. Reproduce the pictures. Allow children to color them and take them home.

**What to Say:**

Some people have special needs. They may have problems seeing, hearing, or walking. Sometimes these people are referred to as specially-abled, disabled, or handicapped. Just like you and me, they need to be able to use the things in our school. Let's take a walk and look around to find out what kinds of things have been specially made to help the disabled children at our school.

# Handicapped Sign

# Visually Impaired Child

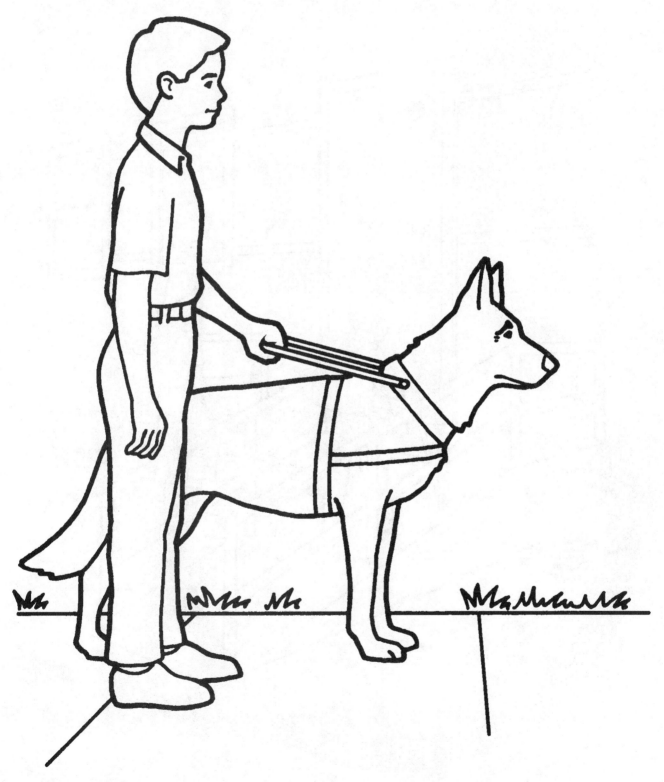

# Orthopedically Handicapped Child

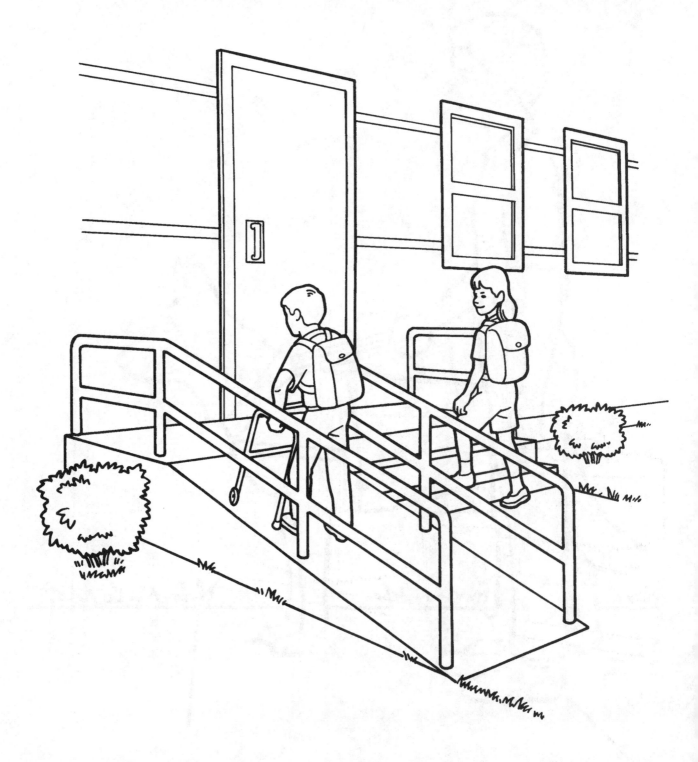

# Adaptive Restroom

# Adaptive School Bus

# Sit-Down Center

## Purpose:

In this activity, children learn to recognize and accommodate for the special needs of physically handicapped students as they help to create a "Sit-Down Center."

**Preparation Time:** One week

## What You Need:

- "Basket" Ball (page 162)
- Bean Bag Toss (page 163)
- Tables adjusted to wheelchair-accessible height
- One or two chairs
- Puzzles
- Games
- Drawing materials
- Other activities (optional)

## What to Do:

In this activity, children help create a center that physically handicapped children would be able to use because the activities are designed to be done sitting down.

Begin by telling children that they are going to help make a "Sit-Down Center." Discuss how physically handicapped children need activities that can be done while sitting. Have children help you gather together the activities that will be placed in the center. Many of these can be activities children are already using, as long as they can be done while sitting. The main idea is to give children an opportunity to understand what is needed for physically handicapped children to be able to use and enjoy activities in the classroom.

## What to Say:

We are going to make a new center in our classroom. It is called a "Sit-Down Center." It will be for children who have trouble walking and standing. All of the activities in this center will need to be the kind that children can do while sitting. Let's think of activities that anyone could do sitting down. *(Provide time for children to brainstorm some activities.)* Now you can help me place those activities in the center. *(Invite volunteers to place activities in the center.)* Why do you think it's important that we have a Sit-Down Center for specially-abled children? *(Have children respond.)*

# "Basket" Ball

## Purpose:

In this activity, children learn how to play a modified game of basketball that can be used for physically handicapped students. This activity is excellent for developing upper-body strength, small and large muscle coordination, and eye-hand coordination.

## Preparation Time: One afternoon

## What You Need:

- Plastic laundry basket or small plastic trash can
- Ten small plastic balls
- One or two chairs depending on the number of players

## What to Do:

This activity is a simple one that children can play immediately and that you can include as part of a Sit-Down Center (page 161). Gather together a plastic laundry basket, two chairs, and 10 small plastic balls. All 10 balls should fit in the laundry basket at one time.

Set up one chair and place the basket several feet away. The idea is to see who can throw all 10 balls into the basket without missing. This activity may prove challenging for preschool-age children. Leave this game as part of your Sit-Down Center so children can play it whenever they have time.

## Variations:

1. Have two sets of balls, each set a different color. Then allow two children to play at the same time and compete against each other.
2. Have the participating child throw the balls wearing a blindfold.
3. After children become successful, move the basket farther away to make the game more challenging again.
4. Divide the class into teams. Have the teams compete against each other. Keep score for each team by awarding a point for every ball thrown in the basket. The winner is the team that has the highest number of points at the end of a period of play that you designate.

## What to Say:

I have a new game for our Sit-Down Center. It's a game we can all play while sitting. Here is what you do: First, set up the basket and the chair so they are a few feet apart. Then, sit in the chair. Next, see if you can throw all 10 balls into the basket without missing. You may also wish to try playing this with a friend and taking turns throwing the balls. See who can throw the most balls into the basket without missing.

# Bean Bag Toss

## Purpose:

In this activity, children learn how to play a modified game that can be used for physically handicapped students. This activity is excellent for developing upper-body strength, small and large muscle coordination, and eye-hand coordination.

## Preparation Time: One afternoon

## What You Need:

- Large box
- Fabric squares, 6" x 6" (15 cm x 15 cm)
- Sewing machine or sewing needle (For adult use only.)
- Thread
- Dried beans

- Scissors
- Craft knife (For adult use only.)
- Poster paint
- Paintbrush
- One or two chairs depending on the number of players

## What to Do:

Before this activity, prepare the bean bags using the dried beans, fabric squares, thread, and a sewing machine or sewing needle. The bean bags can easily be sewn using a machine, or they can be made by hand using a needle. As an alternative, you may prefer to purchase the bean bags. Some teacher supply stores have bean bags you can buy for your classroom.

After the bean bags are prepared, make a target using the large box. Use a craft knife to cut out a circle, a square, and a triangle from the bottom of the box. Then paint the box with poster paint and outline the holes in black poster paint so they are easier for children to see. Place the box close enough to chairs in your Sit-Down Center that children can play by throwing the bean bags into the holes in the box.

## Try these simple games:

- three players, each player picks a shape
- one player, alternates shapes
- teams of three, each team picks one shape for each turn

## What to Say:

I have made a new game for our Sit-Down Center. It is a Bean Bag Toss. Here is how you play the game. Take a bean bag. Then decide which shape you would like to throw the bean bag through. You can choose a circle, square, or triangle. Who can show me the triangle? Who can show me the circle? Who can show me the square? *(Ask volunteers.)* Now let's take turns throwing the bean bags while sitting in these chairs. *(Model the activity for children.)*

# Hearing Impaired

## Purpose:

This activity shows children a mode of communication used by people who are hearing impaired. Children learn to use fingerspelling for the letters of the alphabet and the numbers, 1–10.

**Preparation Time:** Several hours

## What You Need:

- Fingerspelling (pages 165 and 166)
- Poster board
- Glue

## What to Do:

In this activity, children learn the alphabet (a–z) and numbers (1–10) using fingerspelling, a form of manual communication sometimes used by people who are hearing impaired. After children learn fingerspelling, you may wish to introduce them to sign language.

Begin this activity by discussing with children how people who are hearing impaired communicate using sign language and fingerspelling. Explain that some people who cannot hear may not be able to speak either. As a result, they learn to communicate using sign language and fingerspelling. Point out that some people who are hearing impaired are able to read lips in order to understand what another person is saying.

Create posters using copies of the Fingerspelling pictures (pages 165 and 166). Show children the fingerspelling positions. As part of the regular daily routine, have them fingerspell the alphabet while they sing or recite it. You may wish to teach children how to spell their names. Reproduce the fingerspelling pages and provide copies for them to take home. Encourage children to practice their fingerspelling at home, by themselves or with family members.

## What to Say:

Some people are hearing impaired. This means that they have trouble hearing or they cannot hear at all. People who are hearing impaired have a special way of communicating, or talking. Some read lips. This means that they look at the mouth of the person who is speaking to figure out what is being said. Others use sign language and fingerspelling. Some use lipreading and their hands to talk. I am going to teach you fingerspelling. You are going to learn how to say the alphabet and count to ten using your fingers. Let's look at the poster that shows the fingerspelling positions. I will show you how to make a letter, then I want you to make the same letter. *(Model the activity.)*

# Fingerspelling

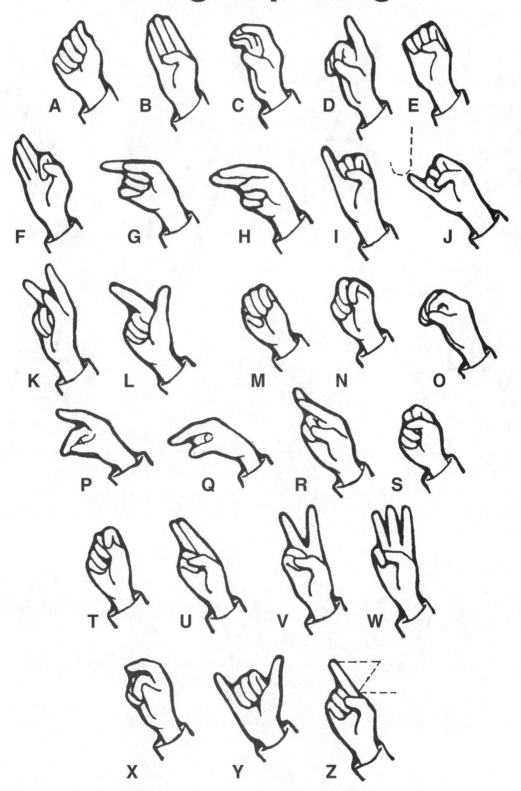

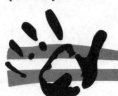

# Fingerspelling *(cont.)*

**1**

**2**

**3**

**4**

**5**

**6**

**7**

**8**

**9**

**10**

# Moving/New Situations

## Section Introduction

## Story

This is a story about Jimmy and his mother moving to a new house in a new city. In a manner that is appropriate and sensitive to youngsters, this story takes a realistic look at the fears and questions most young children have about moving.

## Stick Puppet and Flannelboard Patterns

These patterns (pages 181–186) can be used to help children understand the issues that are emphasized in the story.

## Activities

All of these activities are designed to help children with the transition of moving by giving them information about and insight into the process.

# Children and Change

## Before the Move

Changes, whether they are good or bad, are often stressful. Many children have different ways of facing new situations such as moving. Most of the time parents are occupied with the details of the move and may not think about how traumatic this event might be for their children. Like adults, children must leave behind the security of their home and the comfort of their friends. However, youngsters must also deal with the anxiety of starting at a new school.

As with a divorce, some children may fear that they will be abandoned in the move. It is important to reassure them that no matter what the reasons are for relocating, that they will have a home and there will be someone to care for them. Other children may worry that their "treasured" possessions will be left behind. You may wish to suggest to parents that they allow their children to help pack the toys, books, stuffed animals, etc., to alleviate some of these concerns.

## After the Move

It is easy for children to become overwhelmed on the first day at their new school. If they begin school on the same day as everyone else, they will probably find that there are other new students. However, it is always more difficult for children who move during the school year and come into a classroom where everyone knows everyone else and all of the children are familiar with the daily routine. It is important that teachers and students make the transition for new children as smooth and simple as possible, ensuring that it will be a positive experience.

## In This Book

This book provides a variety of suggestions to help children deal with experiences relating to new situations such as moving. The section begins with a story about a boy named Jimmy who is told by his mother that they are moving (pages 169–180). In the story, Jimmy tells how he feels before and after the move. Stick puppet and flannel board patterns (pages 181–186) are provided for children to role-play the story as well as their own experiences, fears, and concerns. Activities (pages 187–208) are included to help children understand and cope with transitions such as moving.

# Moving Day

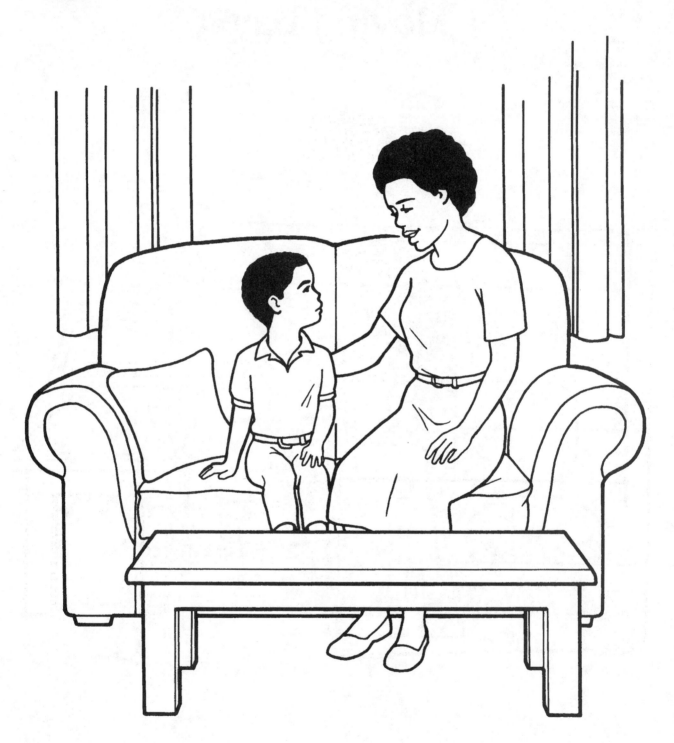

Jimmy was moving.

His mommy told him the news.

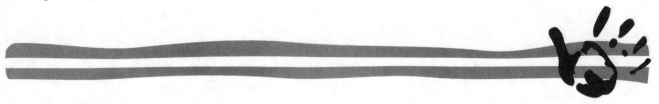

"Honey, we are moving. I have a new job in another city. We will be living in a new house in a new place. You will have a new school," said Mommy.

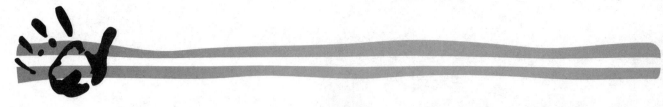

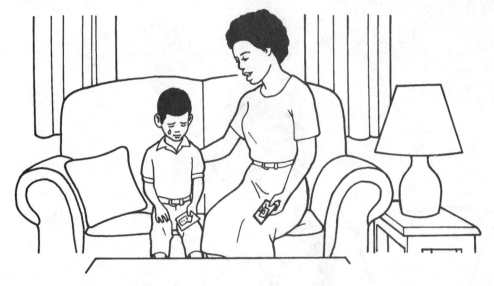

"A new house?  A new school?  I don't want to move!"
Jimmy cried.

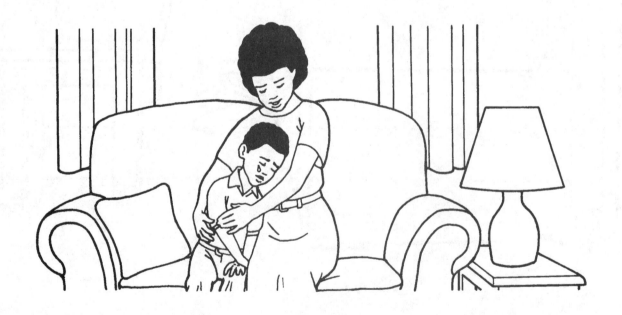

"I know it will be hard to move away from our house and
all our friends," Mommy told Jimmy.

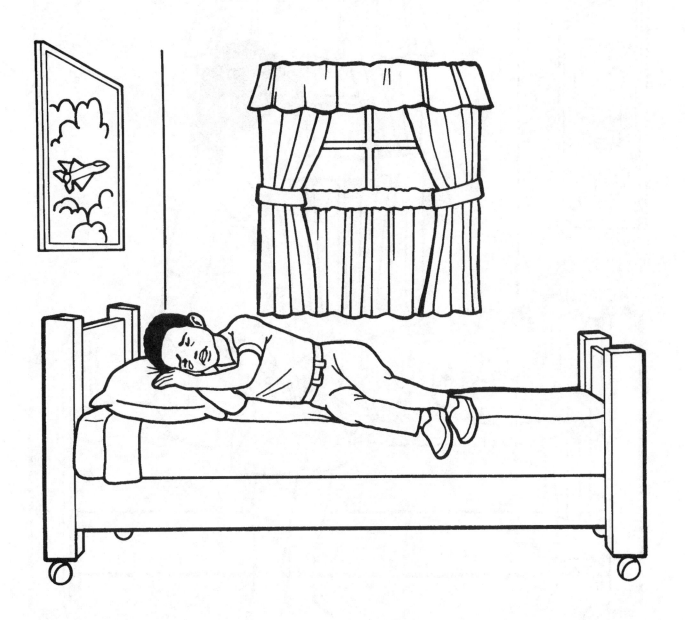

Jimmy was moving. He had to move. His mother had a new job in a new city. He would have a new house and a new school.

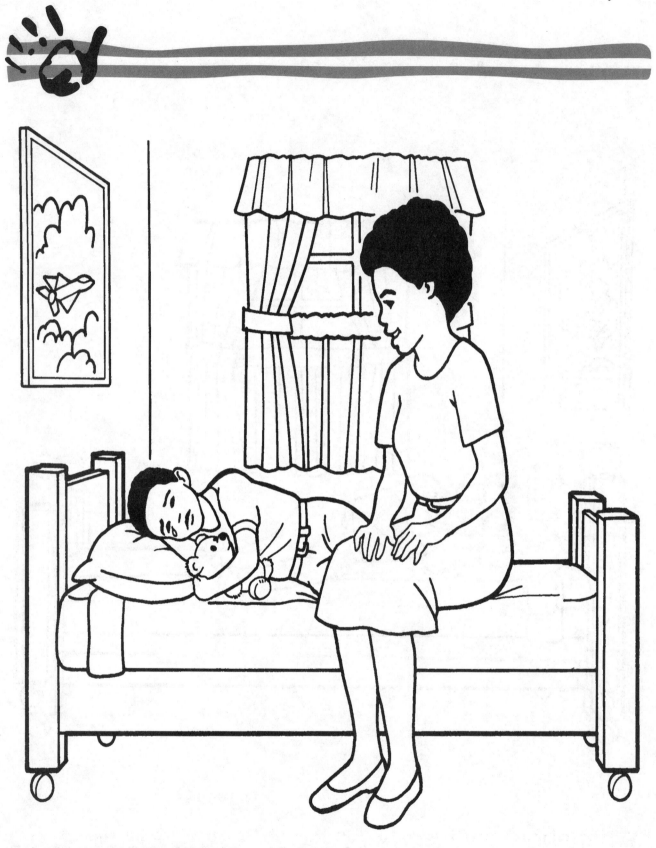

"But what about my toys?" Jimmy asked.

"You can take all of them," said Mommy.

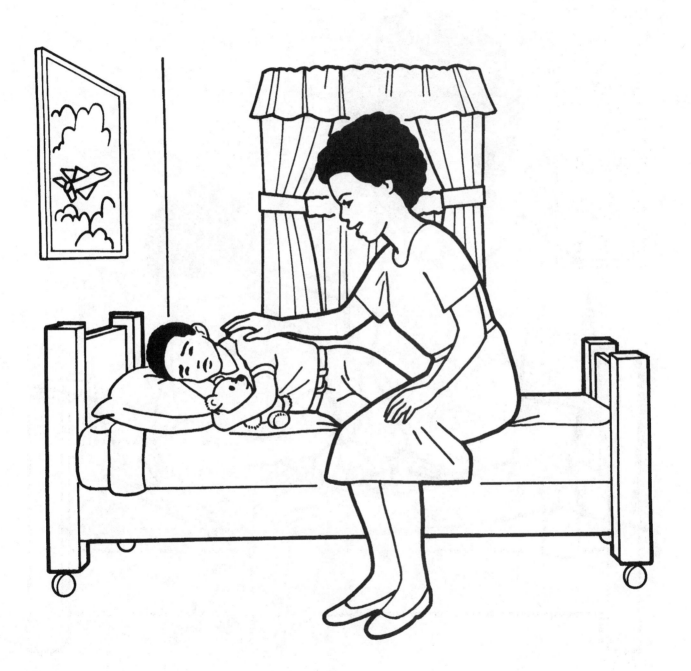

"What about my friends?" asked Jimmy.

"You can write, call, or visit them," answered his mommy.

The next day, Jimmy's mommy helped him write the names and phone numbers of his friends in a special address book. Then Jimmy said good-bye to all his friends.

A few days later, Mommy asked Jimmy to help put his toys in boxes. He did.

Soon the movers came and took all the boxes away to the new house. Then the movers lifted the furniture into the moving van. They worked very hard.

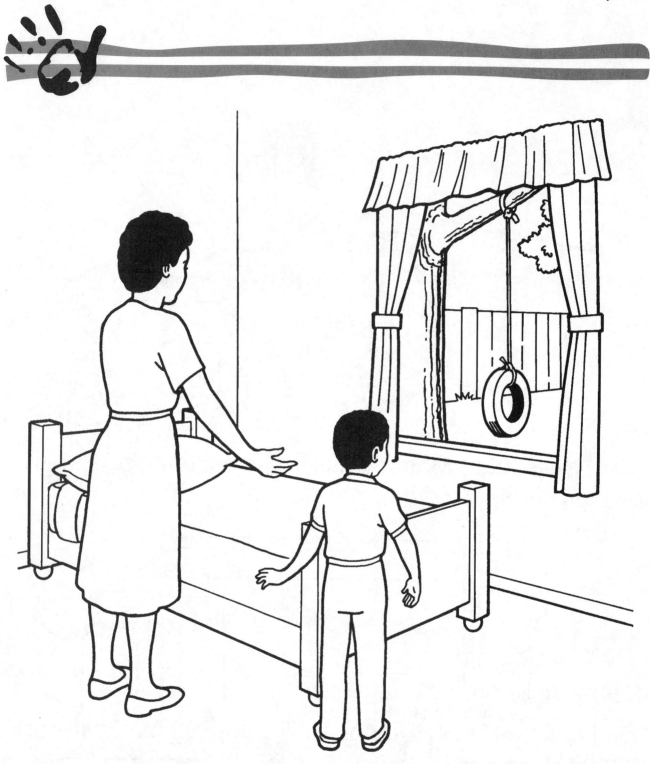

Finally, Jimmy and his mother started living in the new house.

Jimmy noticed that his new room had a big window and the yard had a swing. He thought to himself that maybe moving wouldn't be so bad.

Jimmy walked outside his new house.

"Hi, I'm Chris," yelled a boy with a puppy. "What's your name?"

"I'm Jimmy. This is my new house. I just moved here," he replied.

"Great," said Chris. "Do you want to play with me?"

"Sure. Let me ask my mom first."

Jimmy ran inside to ask his mom.

"Of course you can play with your new friend, Jimmy," said his mommy. "Just stay on the lawn where I can see you."

"Mom," said Jimmy, "I still miss my old friends, but it will be fun to have new friends, too."

"I know what you mean," she said as he ran out the door to play.

# Stick Puppet and Flannelboard Patterns

**Jimmy**

# Stick Puppet and Flannelboard Patterns *(cont.)*

### Jimmy's Mom

# Stick Puppet and Flannelboard Patterns *(cont.)*

**Chris**

# Stick Puppet and Flannelboard
# Patterns *(cont.)*

**Moving Van**

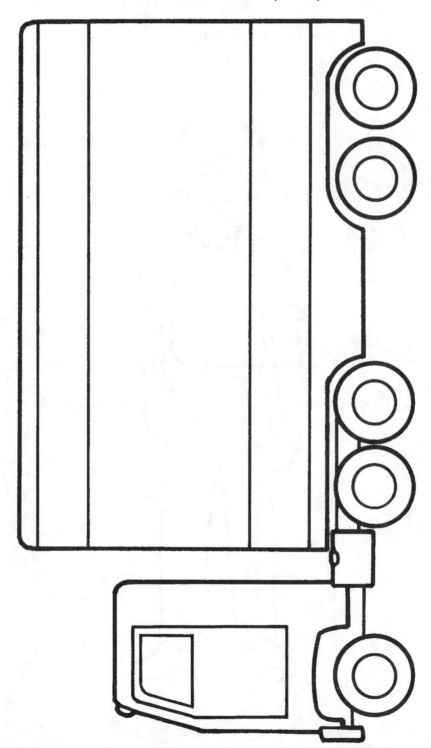

# Stick Puppet and Flannelboard Patterns *(cont.)*

## Movers

# Stick Puppet and Flannelboard Patterns *(cont.)*

### Moving Boxes and Suitcases

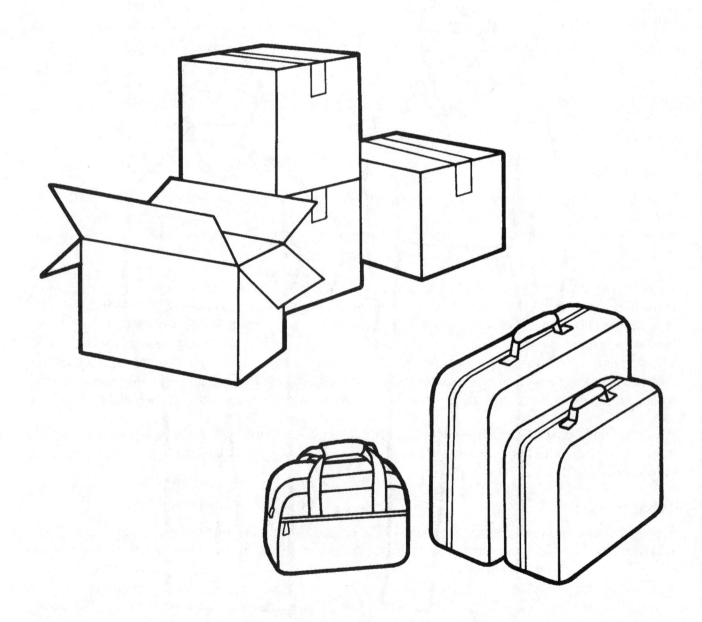

# Keeping in Touch

## Purpose:

This activity gives children an opportunity to make address books in which they can write their friends' addresses and phone numbers. This will help them stay in contact with their friends even after moving to a new home.

## Preparation Time: One hour

## What You Need:

- My Address Book (pages 188 and 189)
- Stapler
- Art supplies
- Pencils or pens
- Variety of address books (optional)

MY
ADDRESS
BOOK

## What to Do:

Begin this activity by reading aloud "Moving Day" (pages 169–180). Discuss with children their experiences with moving to new homes, new towns, and new schools. Ask them to share their feelings. Invite them to tell what was the easiest thing about moving. Then ask them to tell what was the hardest thing about moving.

After reading the story, talk with children about what it is like to move. Point out that Jimmy's mother helps him write down his friends' addresses and phone numbers so he can keep in touch with them. Ask children how they can keep in touch with their old friends. Show them some address books if you have some available. Ask them to note what is the same about the books. Lead students to conclude that they have spaces for people's names, addresses, and phone numbers. Tell children that they are going to get to make their own address books for this activity. Prepare the address books ahead of time by stapling together one cover (page 189) and several inside pages (page 188) for each child.

As part of this activity, you may wish to include a discussion about how to make new friends after you move. Encourage children to brainstorm a list of ways to make new friends. Record their responses on butcher paper or the chalkboard.

## What to Say:

Today I am going to read you a story about a little boy and his mother who move to a new place. You will hear how he feels about moving and what he is worried about. You will also hear what happens after he moves. *(Read aloud "Moving Day.")* Now that we have heard the story, let's talk about it. *(Lead a discussion about the story.)* Jimmy's mother gives him an address book and helps him write down the addresses and phone numbers of the friends. Today, you are going to make address books so we can share our numbers. You will have your very own address book to take home.

# My Address Book

| NAME: | NAME: |
|---|---|
| ADDRESS: | ADDRESS: |
| | |
| PHONE: | PHONE: |
| NAME: | NAME: |
| ADDRESS: | ADDRESS: |
| | |
| PHONE: | PHONE: |
| NAME: | NAME: |
| ADDRESS: | ADDRESS: |
| | |
| PHONE: | PHONE: |
| NAME: | NAME: |
| ADDRESS: | ADDRESS: |
| | |
| PHONE: | PHONE: |

# My Address Book *(cont.)*

MY
ADDRESS
BOOK

# Home Decorator

## Purpose:

In this activity, children use their imaginations to pretend that they are home decorators. They can imagine their new houses and use the game pieces and room floor plan to decorate their own rooms. You may wish to challenge children to make game pieces of their own if they would like different furnishings such as a bunk bed.

## Preparation Time: Two afternoons

## What You Need:

- Room Floor Plan (page 193)
- Game Pieces (pages 191 and 192)
- Laminating film or clear contact paper
- Poster board or card stock
- Glue
- Markers
- Scissors
- Cardboard boxes or large envelopes with brads, one for each game

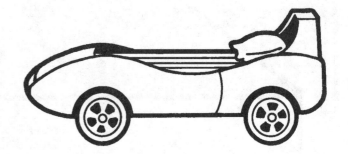

## What to Do:

Before using this activity in your classroom, you will need to prepare the Game Pieces and the Room Floor Plan. Reproduce pages 191–193. Enlarge the Room Floor Plan to accommodate Game Pieces. Cut out and color the Game Pieces. Then mount the Game Pieces and Room Floor Plan on poster board or card stock. After gluing and pressing the pieces, laminate or use clear contact paper to cover them.

Place each completed game in a cardboard box or large envelope with a brad. This will make the pieces easy to store so that the game can be used again and again.

Begin this activity by discussing with children about what it is like to move to a new house and have a new bedroom. Invite children who have had experiences with moving to a new home share what it was like for them. Then model the game by showing children the Game Pieces and talking about what each is and where it might go in a room. Place the game in your Activity Center. Encourage children to take turns playing the game. You may wish to allow children to make additional game pieces to add to their floor plans.

## What to Say:

Moving means that you leave the place where you are living now to go live in a new place. You might have a new room that will be all yours, or you might have to share your room with another person in your family. Has anyone ever moved to a new home? What was it like? *(Lead a discussion about this.)* Let's all look at a new game. Use your imagination, the Game Pieces, and the Room Floor Plan to design your new room the way you would like for it to be.

# Game Pieces

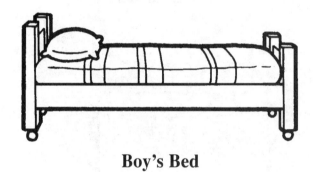

**Boy's Bed**

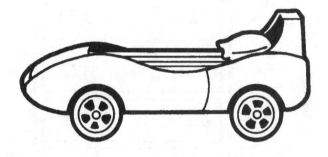

**Boy's Bed**

**Girl's Bed**

**Girl's Bed**

# Game Pieces *(cont.)*

**Chest of Drawers**

**Toy Box**

**Books**

**Toys**

# Room Floor Plan

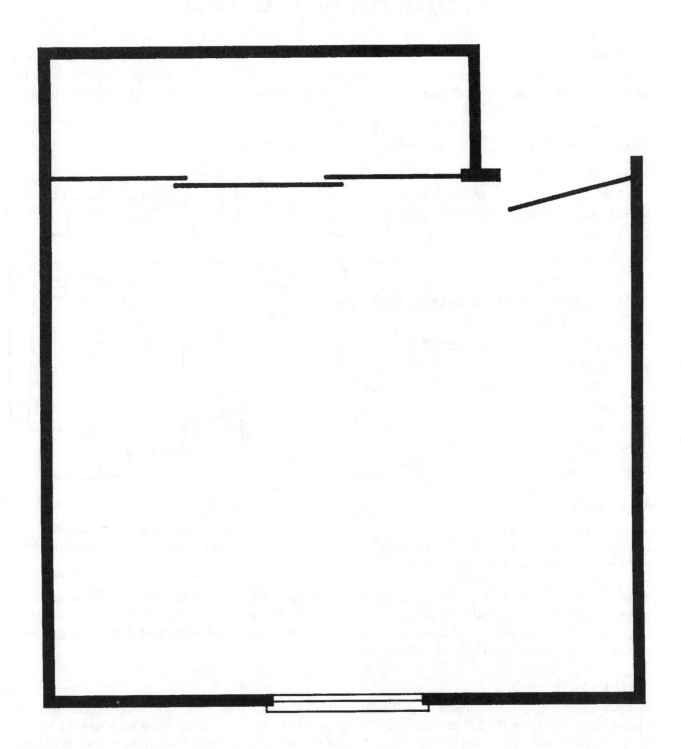

# Super Students Moving Company Center

## Purpose:

In this activity, children get a chance to role-play being movers using their own Super Students Moving Company Center. This activity allows children to be comfortable with the many aspects of moving by becoming make-believe movers.

## Preparation Time: Several afternoons

## What You Need:

- Moving Center Setup (page 195)
- Moving Company Office Sign (page 196)
- Mover's Hat (page 197)
- Cardboard boxes
- Masking tape
- Large black crayons or markers
- Various items to pack
- Wagon
- Clipboard
- Paper
- Pen
- Desk
- Chair
- Telephone

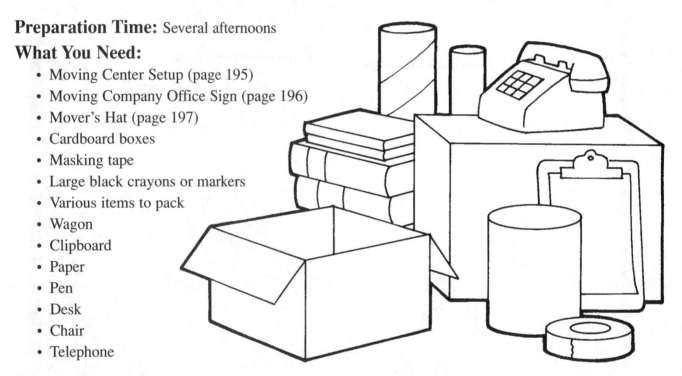

## What to Do:

In this activity, you prepare a Super Students Moving Company Center in your classroom and your children become movers. Children role-play a real-life situation in order to become more comfortable with their own feelings and expectations.

Prepare for this activity by reproducing pages 195–197, gathering the supplies needed and creating the center (page 195). It is possible to collect most of the materials you need from your classroom. You may also wish to ask parents and local grocers for donations. Children can pack and move classroom objects, such as those found in a Kitchen Center.

## What to Say:

We have a new center in our classroom. It's called the Super Students Moving Company. You will all get a chance to be movers. Let me show you around the moving office area. We have a moving truck, boxes and tape, and a clipboard with paper and a pen for invoices and important moving papers. Here is the desk, chair, and telephone for the moving office. Who would like to be the first movers?

# Moving Center Setup

This shows one suggestion for how to arrange your Moving Center. You may need to adapt it, depending on the furniture and amount of space you have available in your classroom. Keep the tape, large black crayons or markers, clipboard, paper, and pen at the desk.

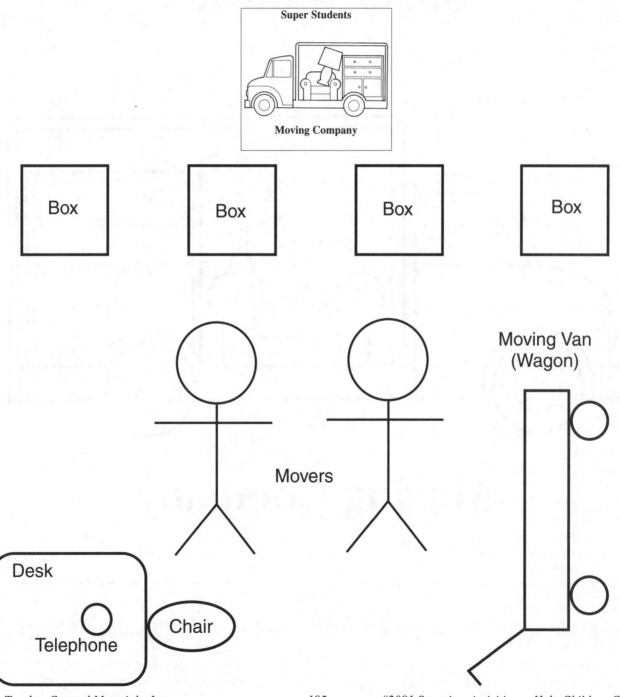

# Moving Company Office Sign

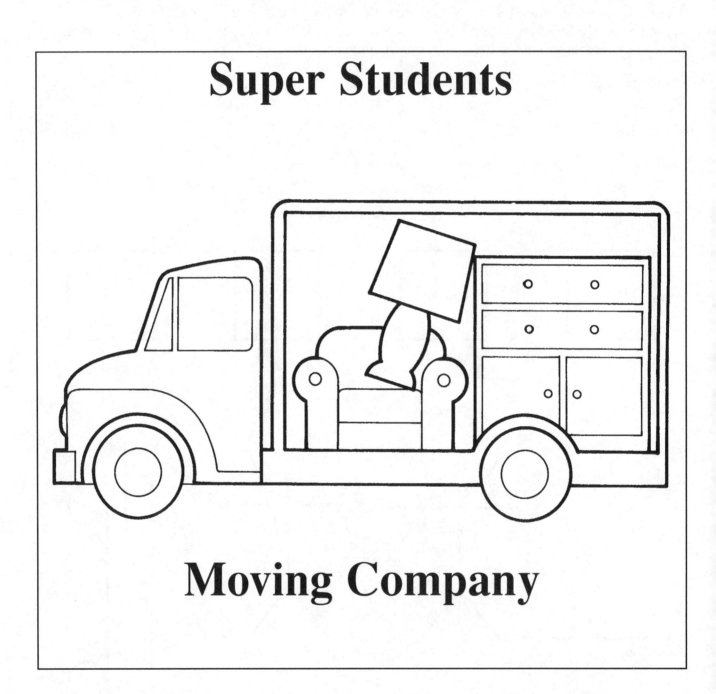

# Mover's Hat

Use the following directions for each mover's hat.

1. Reproduce the visor pattern onto tagboard. Cut it out. Fold it along the dashed lines.
2. Measure and cut a 4" (10.5 cm) wide band of tagboard.
   The length will vary depending on the size of the child's head.
3. Use tape to connect the visor to the band.
4. Tape or staple the band to fit the child's head.

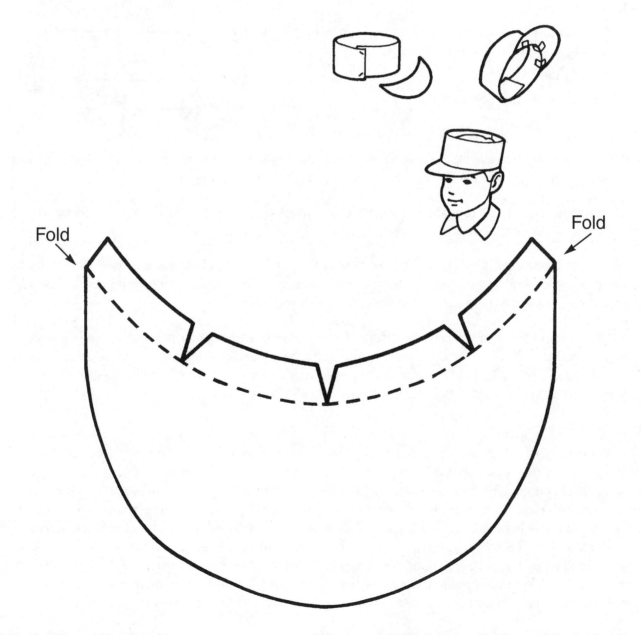

# Packing Game

## Purpose:

The purpose of this game is to give children an opportunity to think about all of the things they would take with them when or if they move. They must decide how they should pack all of their belonging into a "moving truck." In addition, using the packing labels helps children learn to recognize letters and words.

## Preparation Time: One day

## What You Need:

- Plain large wooden blocks or cardboard boxes in various sizes
- Packing Labels (pages 199–203)
- Glue or tape
- Standard-size children's wagon

## What to Do:

In this activity, children use labeled blocks or boxes that represent the various items in a home to decide how these items should be packed into a wagon that represents a moving truck.

Prepare for this activity by reproducing the Packing Labels (pages 199–203). Use glue or tape to secure these to the blocks or boxes before presenting the game to children.

Then, during circle time, show children how to play the game. Read aloud each of the labels to help children become familiar with them. Then discuss what each item is. Encourage children to tell why it is important for them to have these items in their new houses.

You will also find that children have a variety of other objects around their homes that they feel are important to them. You may wish to make additional labels based on their requests. Be sure to discuss how to categorize the items into groups. Set up this activity for children to use during self-directed play time, so each child can have a chance to pack the "moving truck."

## What to Say:

I have made a new game. It's a packing game where we pretend that we are moving to a new home. We will pretend that these labeled blocks/boxes have the things we own in side of them. I have put packing labels on the blocks/boxes so you will know what's inside. First, I will read aloud the words on the blocks/boxes. Then you can tell me why you think it is important for you to take each of these things to your new home. *(Read the packing labels and have children tell what purpose each item serves and why it would be important to have.)* Now you will get to take turns packing the "moving truck" which is the wagon. What kinds of things need to go into a moving truck first? *(Have children name items that they would put into the truck first. Then ask them to explain their reasoning. Lead children to conclude that it is important to place the heaviest and largest items in first.)*

# Packing Labels

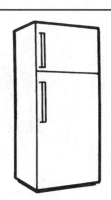

**Refrigerator**

**Washer**

**Dryer**

**Microwave**

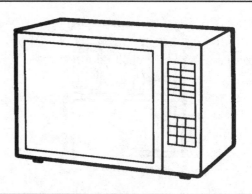

# Packing Labels *(cont.)*

 **Dishes, Knives, Forks, Spoons**

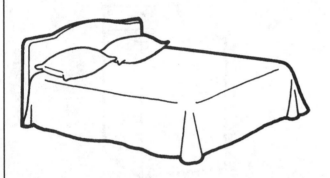 **Bed**

**Crib**

 **Bookcase**

# Packing Labels *(cont.)*

 **Books and Toys**

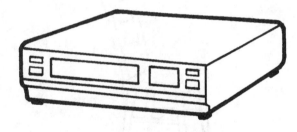 **VCR**

 **Pots and Pans**

  **Clothes**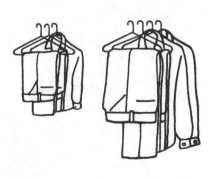

# Packing Labels *(cont.)*

 **Dresser**

**Chair**

**Coffee Table**

**Desk**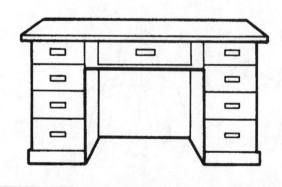

# Packing Labels *(cont.)*

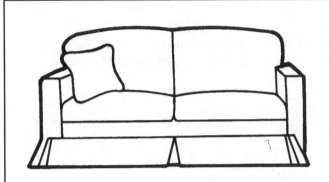

**Sofa**

**Kitchen Table**

**TV**

**Computer**

# My House

## Purpose:

In this activity, children have the opportunity to select pictures of homes that are most similar to their own type of homes. Then they individualize their pictures and add them to a mural neighborhood.

## Preparation Time: Several hours

## What You Need:

- Large piece of butcher paper
- Art supplies
- Tape
- Glue
- Stick pins
- Crayons
- Scissors
- Types of Homes (pages 205–208)
- Construction paper

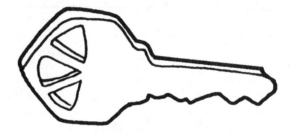

## What to Do:

Provide children with the opportunity to create homes that resemble their own. Then they add them to a mural neighborhood. Begin this activity by hanging up the butcher paper for the mural. You will need to decide now much of the mural you would like to complete and present to your children at the onset of the activity. Some teachers prefer to use the construction paper to make trees, streets, etc., to prepare a whole neighborhood and have children add only their homes. Others prefer to leave a lot of the neighborhood art to the children. As you are preparing the mural, remember to leave spaces for the houses.

Have children select homes from the various Types of Homes (pages 205–208) that are similar to the places where they live. Ask them to complete their homes by coloring and decorating their pictures. Invite each child to pick a place for his or her home in the neighborhood shown on the mural. Help children add their homes to the mural. The result will be a darling mural that will make children feel good about their homes.

## What to Say:

We are going to make a mural, which is like a very large picture. This will be a mural of a neighborhood. As you can see, I have already started to put some things, such as trees and streets, in our neighborhood. First, look through these pictures to find a home that looks something like the home you are living in right now. *(Allow children to pick their homes.)* Color and decorate your picture. *(Allow children to color and decorate.)* Now we are ready to add your homes to the mural. *(Help children attach their homes to the mural.)*

# Types of Homes

# Types of Homes *(cont.)*

# Types of Homes *(cont.)*

# Types of Homes (cont.)

# Loneliness

## Section Introduction

Feeling of Loneliness (page 210)

## Story

"Felix, the Lonely Caterpillar" (pages 211–226)

This story is about a little caterpillar named Felix who is lonely. With the help of a friend, he learns a way to get over his feelings of loneliness.

## Stick Puppet and Flannelboard Patterns

These patterns (pages 227–229) can be used to help children understand the issues that are emphasized in the story.

## Activities

- Contemplation Cave (page 230)
- Making a Friendship Caterpillar (pages 231–233)
- Making and Keeping Friends (page 234)
- Affirmation Jar (pages 235 and 236)
- Class Book (pages 237–239)

All of these activities reinforce children's ability to find ways to cope with loneliness while learning how to enjoy spending time alone. They help children realize that family members and friends can provide emotional support.

# Feelings of Loneliness

Teachers should assure children that everyone feels lonely at times. Even young children know what it is like to feel lonely. Loneliness does not necessarily affect people only when they are alone. People can also feel lonely when surrounded by friends and/or family members. Educators can help children recognize the difference between being alone and being lonely. Understanding this difference and being able to alleviate feelings of loneliness while still enjoying doing things alone are necessary life skills. It is important to give children strategies to cope with their loneliness.

## Depression

Feelings of loneliness can lead to the more serious problem of depression. Children who are depressed may exhibit some or all of the following symptoms.

1. They lose interest in activities that they used to enjoy. They lack motivation and often have a negative attitude. They may have short attention spans or are easily distracted.

2. Their appetite changes. They either eat almost nothing or they eat constantly. Foods that used to be their favorites are no longer appealing.

3. Their sleep habits change. They may have difficulty sleeping and seem lethargic when awake or they may sleep all of the time.

4. They may appear to be physically drained. They have short attention spans and are often too tired to participate in normal activities.

5. They tend to withdraw from others and dislike themselves. They do not believe that they have any friends. They may be especially susceptible to peer pressure because they want to be accepted by their peers.

6. They tend to have an overwhelming feeling of sadness. They feel helpless and worry about things they cannot control.

7. They have difficulty concentrating, so they do poorly in school and often cannot complete household chores. They may have problems sitting still long enough to do activities.

8. They spend a great deal of time thinking about death and/or suicide.

9. They may become behavior problems at home and at school.

10. They may complain of aches and pains on a regular basis.

## In This Book

This book provides a variety of suggestions to help children deal with experiences relating to loneliness. The section begins with a story about loneliness (pages 211–226), giving even very young children some basic information about what loneliness is and how to combat it. Stick puppet and flannel board patterns (pages 227–229) are provided for children to role-play the story as well as their own experiences, fears, and concerns. Activities (pages 230–239) are included to help children understand and cope with feelings of loneliness.

# Felix, the Lonely Caterpillar

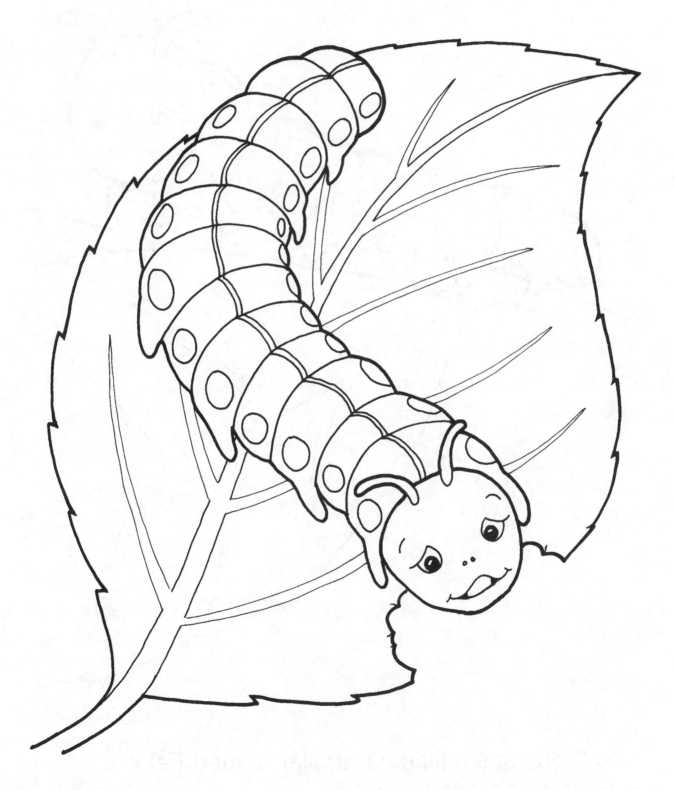

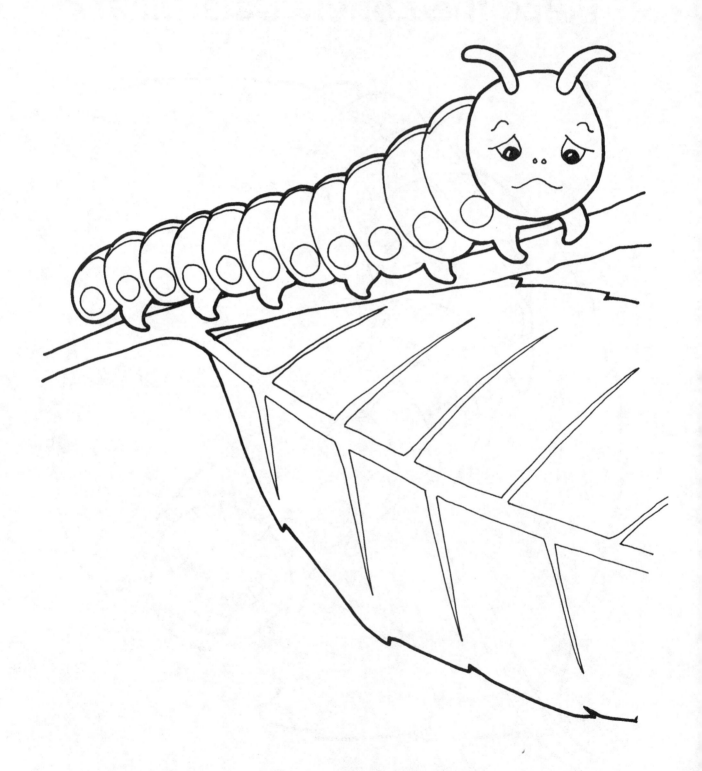

# Once there was a little caterpillar named Felix.

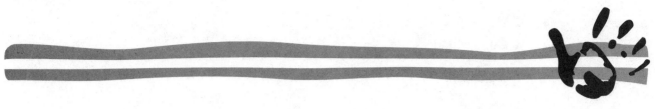

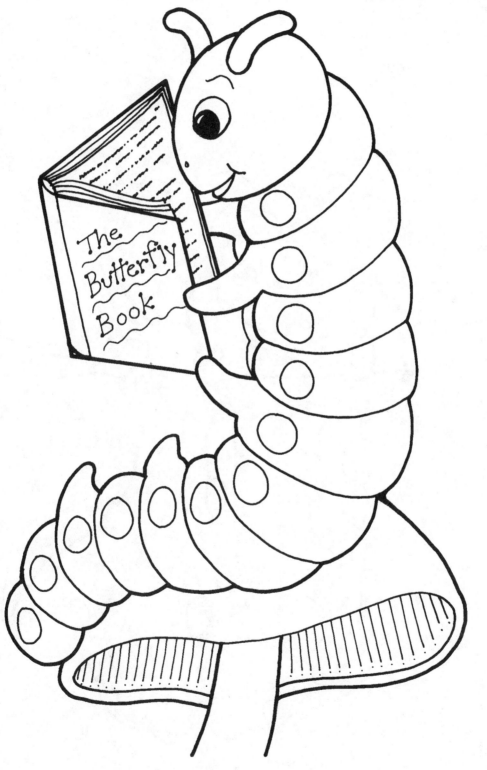

# Sometimes he liked being alone.

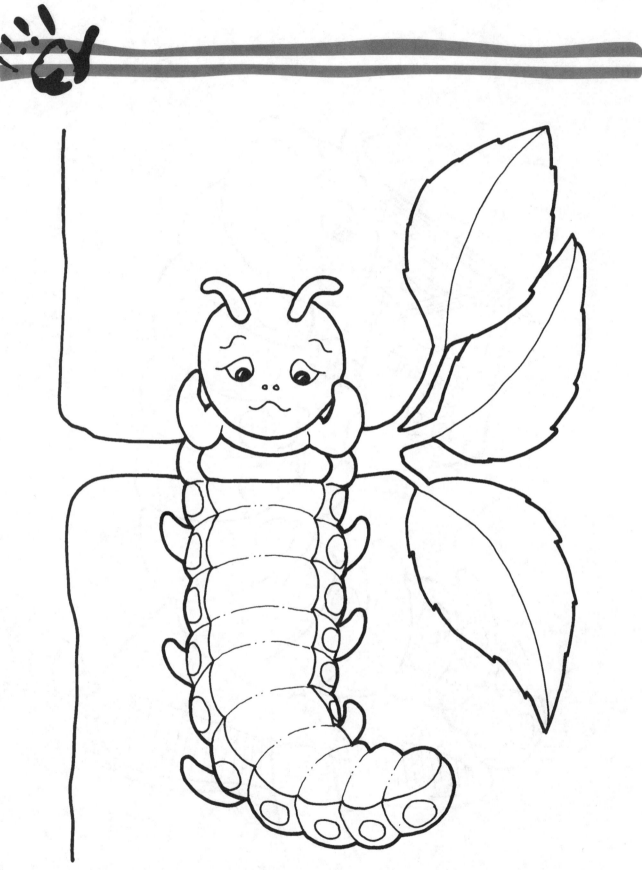

But now he felt lonely when he was by himself.

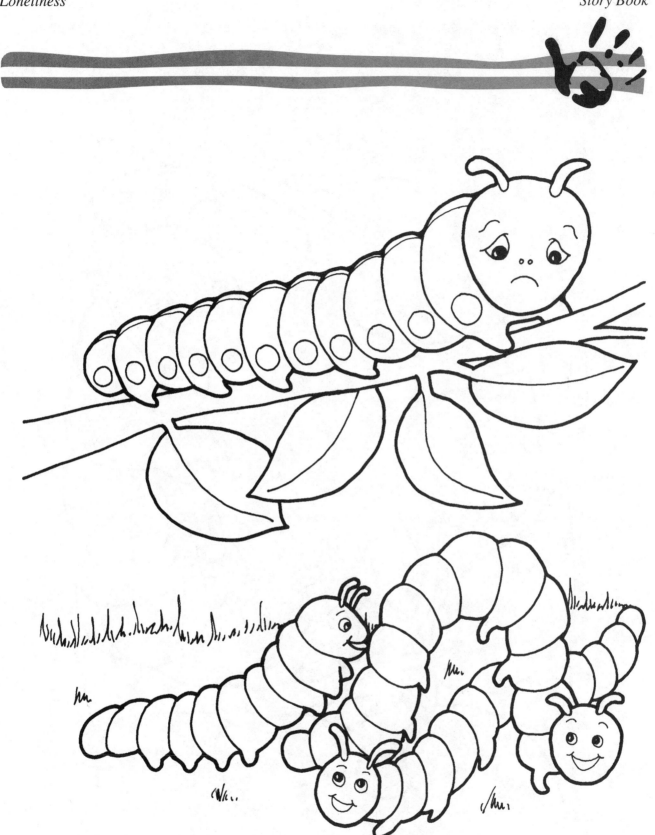

He usually liked playing with his caterpillar friends. But even though he wasn't alone, he still felt lonely.

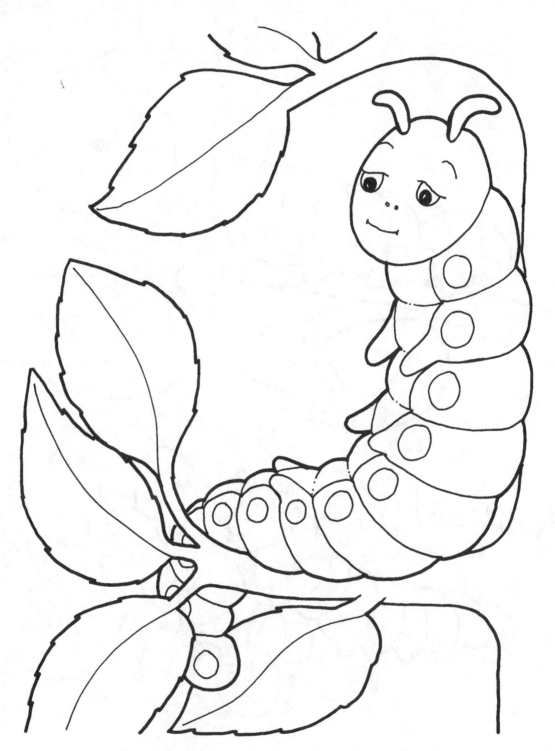

Every night, Felix sat by himself on a twig at the top of a tree.

He stared at the moon and sighed, "How can I stop feeling lonely?"

# Felix decided to ask his friend Lilly for help.

Lilly saw how sad Felix was.  She told him that everyone
feels lonely at times.

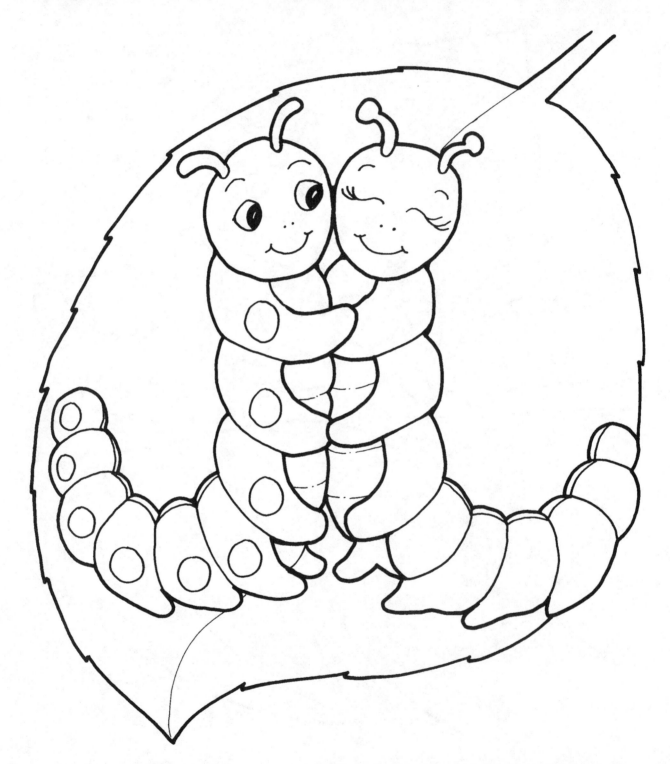

Felix felt a little better. He thought he was the only one who felt lonely.

Lilly told Felix that he should try to do something new.
Then maybe he wouldn't have time to feel so lonely.

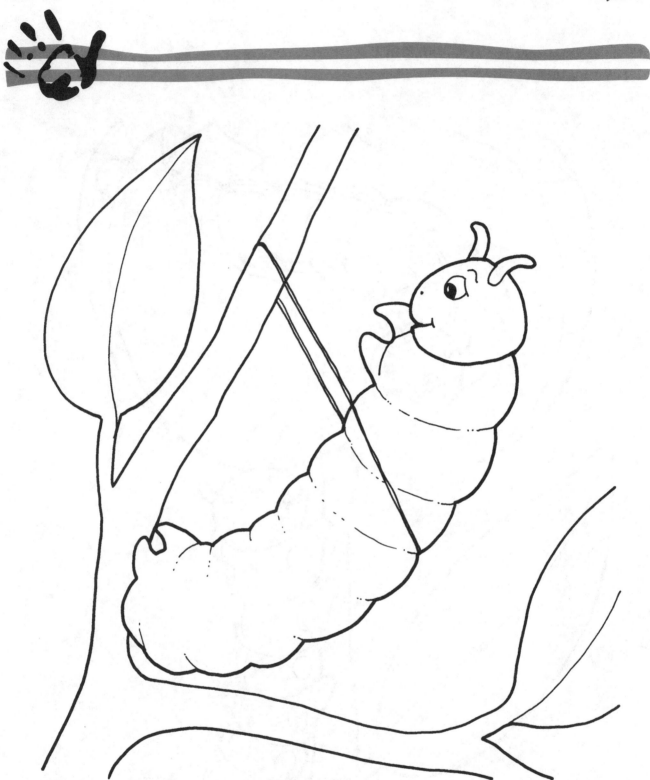

Felix thought and thought about what he should do.
Suddenly he decided to spin a cocoon. It was fun
spinning the cocoon. Before Felix knew it, he didn't feel
lonely anymore.

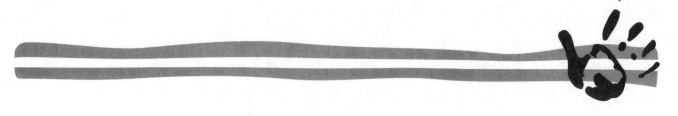

Then one sunny day, when the leaves sparkled with dew, Felix slowly climbed out of his cocoon. He stretched his wings and smiled. "I'm a butterfly!" he exclaimed.

# Felix took a look around and saw other butterflies.

"Hello!" he shouted as he waved at the other butterflies. The other butterflies waved and smiled at him. Then one butterfly flew over to Felix. It was Lilly. She said, "Join us."

Felix did, and he was very happy. The next time Felix feels lonely, he knows he can help himself by doing something new.

# Stick Puppet and Flannelboard Patterns

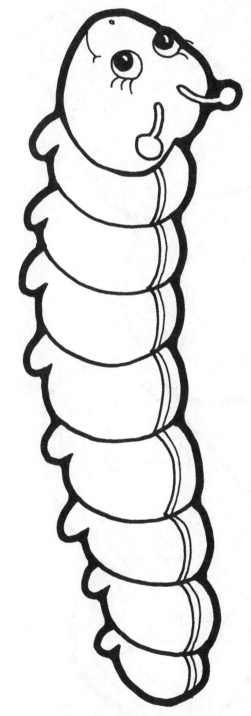

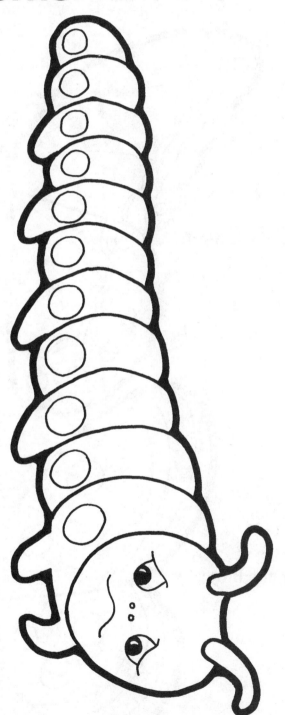

**Lilly, the Caterpillar**                    **Felix, the Caterpillar**

227

# Stick Puppet and
# Flannelboard Patterns *(cont.)*

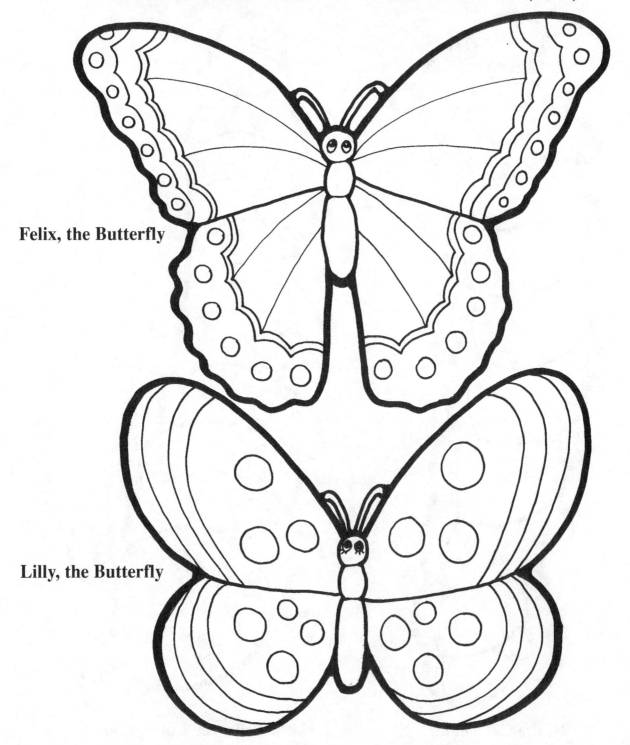

**Felix, the Butterfly**

**Lilly, the Butterfly**

# Stick Puppet and
# Flannelboard Patterns *(cont.)*

**Other Butterflies**                        **Leaf**

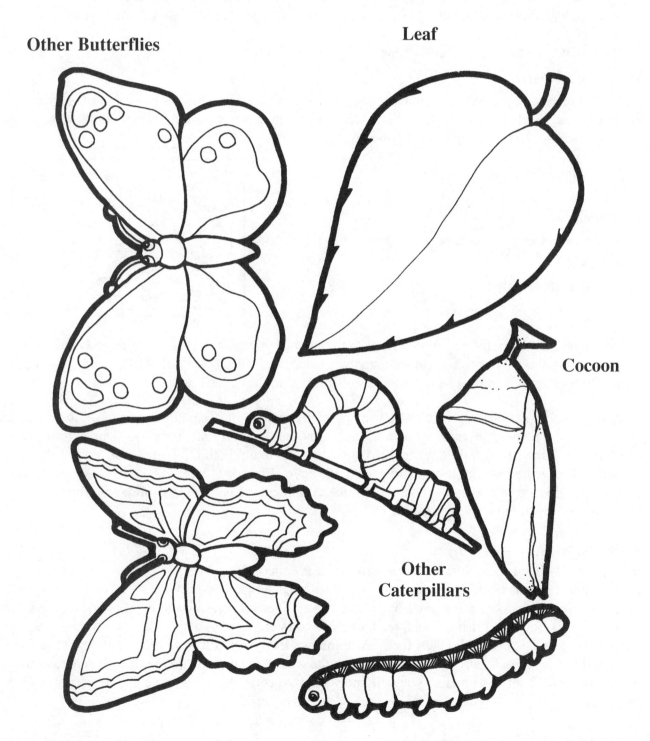

**Cocoon**

**Other
Caterpillars**

# Contemplation Cave

## Purpose:

The purpose of this activity is to create a Contemplation Cave where individual children can sit and think, read, listen to music or story tapes, or daydream and enjoy being alone for a little while.

## Preparation Time: Several afternoons

## What You Need:

**Note:** Use materials you have on hand, such as a large cardboard refrigerator box or short, stable bookcases and sheets of butcher paper. The idea is to create a private space, something like a reading nook, where children can spend time by themselves.

- Reading lamp
- Pillows
- Small bookcase or basket full of books
- Tape recorder and music or story tapes
- Timer
- Posters (optional)

## What to Do:

Before beginning this activity, you will need to find a place in your classroom where you can create a Contemplation Cave. You can use almost anything you have on hand to do this. The area should be a place where children can enjoy a few minutes of solitude to think, look at books, or listen to tapes.

After the Contemplation Cave is ready to use, tell children about it. Explain that the cave is a place for children to have some quiet time by themselves. Point out that everyone has to be alone at times and that this is nothing to be afraid of or feel sad about. Stress that it is fun to spend time alone enjoying oneself. Then invite children to take turns using the cave. Provide a timer to be sure that every child gets a turn. Be sure to change the books and tapes on a regular basis so the children will have new materials to use while they are inside the cave.

## What to Say:

We have a new place to explore in our classroom. It is called a Contemplation Cave. The word *contemplation* means thinking quietly. This cave is a special place where you can go to spend some time alone so you can learn to enjoy being by yourself. There is no reason to be afraid or feel sad when you are alone. You may wish to think, read, or listen to music or story tapes. It's nice to have some time alone each day, even if it is just for a few minutes. Everyone will get a turn inside the cave, but you will have to wait patiently while others are in the cave. Be sure you do not disturb someone who is in the cave. I will set this timer so you will know when to come out of the cave and let someone else have a turn.

# Making a Friendship Caterpillar

## Purpose:

The purpose of this art activity is to help children understand the process of making new friends.  It also helps them realize that they have a number of friends they can count on if they feel lonely.

## Preparation Time: Two hours

## What You Need:

- Friendship Caterpillar (pages 232 and 233)
- Construction paper or card stock
- One-hole punch
- Brads
- Glue
- Art supplies, including crayons or markers
- Two pipe cleaners

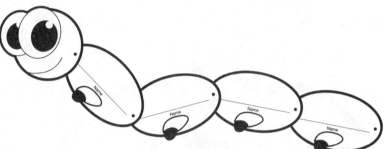

## What to Do:

Before this activity, prepare a sample caterpillar to show children.  Then prepare an Art Center for the caterpillar project.  You may wish to cut out the caterpillar patterns (page 232 and 233) ahead of time since this may be frustrating for some children.

Begin by reading aloud the story "Felix, the Lonely Caterpillar" (pages 211–226).  Discuss with children what happened to Felix.

Next model how to make the Friendship Caterpillar.  Ask children to think of their friends' names.  Point out that they can include family members, too.  Then help children write the names and attach the sections to their caterpillars.  You may wish to enlist the help of parent volunteers or older students for this project.  Encourage children to add more sections to their caterpillars as they make new friends.  The result will be cute paper caterpillars that will grow as the children's lists of friends grow.

## What to Say:

I am going to read you a story entitled, "Felix, the Lonely Caterpillar."  After I finish reading this story, we will talk about what happened to Felix.  *(Lead a class discussion.)*  We all have friends.  If we need or want more friends, we can learn how to make them.  How do you make a new friend?  What does it feel like to be a good friend?  Why is it important to have friends?  Today we are going to make a Friendship Caterpillar in the Art Center.  Think of your friends' names.  I will help you write their names on the sections of the caterpillar.  Then we will use a hole punch and brads to attach the sections to the caterpillar.  *(Model how to make the caterpillar.  Then show what it will look like when it is completed.)*  This is what your caterpillars will look like when you are finished.

# Friendship Caterpillar

Reproduce pages 232 and 233 on construction paper or cardstock. Make one copy of page 232 for each child. Reproduce the caterpillar sections on page 233, making a large number so children can use as many as they need. You may wish to cut out the caterpillar patterns ahead of time. Help children write their friends' names on the sections. Punch the holes where indicated. Use brads to connect the pieces. Ask children to decorate their caterpillars. Use glue to attach pipe cleaners as antennae. Allow the glue to dry. Display the caterpillars. Encourage children to attach additional sections to their caterpillars as they make new friends.

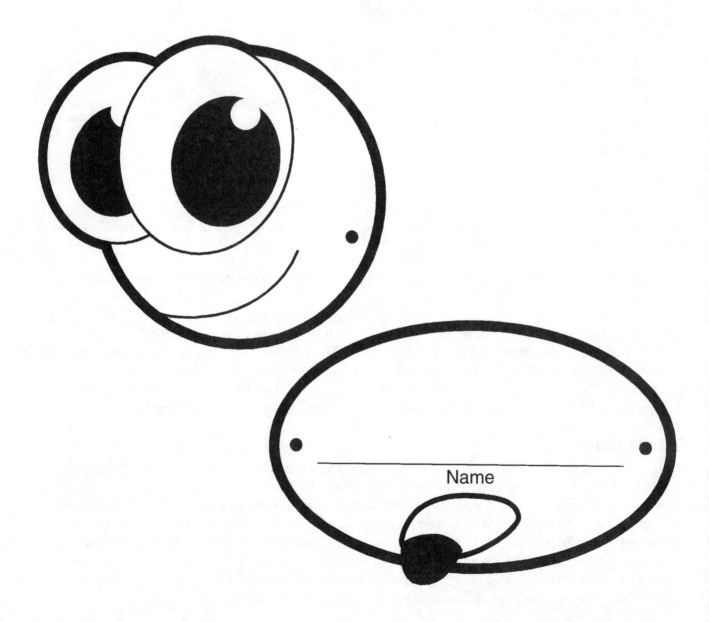

Name

# Friendship Caterpillar *(cont.)*

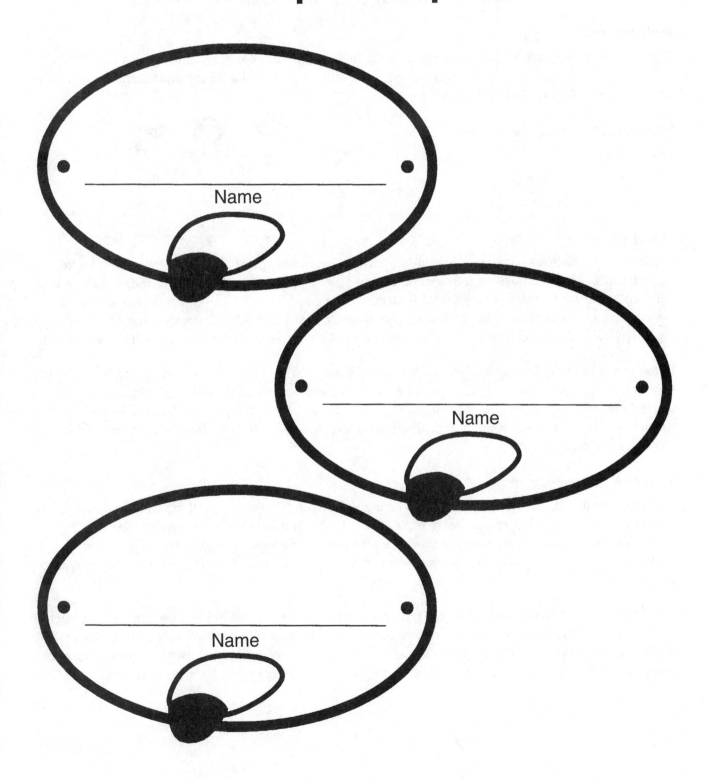

Name

Name

Name

# Making and Keeping Friends

## Purpose:

The purpose of this activity is to give children the feeling that they can learn how to make and keep friends by the way they choose to treat others. This activity gives children the understanding that they have the power to form lasting friendships.

## Preparation Time: One hour
## What You Need:

- Large piece of butcher paper
- Wide-tipped marker

## What to Do:

In this activity, children have an opportunity to discuss friendships and brainstorm a list of ways to make friends. This is a positive step for children in several ways. They have the chance to talk to other children and share their ideas about what it takes to be a good friend. They begin to realize they have the ability to make friends. They can make friends more easily once they learn the process. This is especially helpful for children who feel that they do not have friends or for children who tend to be shy.

Begin this activity by talking to children during circle time. You may wish to read the story "Felix, the Lonely Caterpillar," or just begin a discussion about the importance of friends. Ask children to tell about some of the ways they have made friends. Write their ideas on a piece of butcher paper. Display the list in your classroom. Read it with children on a regular basis to help them remember the different strategies for making friends.

## What to Say:

We are going to talk about what it means to be a good friend. Can anyone tell me what makes a person a good friend? *(Ask volunteers to share their ideas. If children have difficulty getting started, you might need to provide a few examples such as a friend may be someone who is helpful, a friend is someone who is kind, a friend is someone who is fun to be with, or a friend is someone who cares about you.)*

Now think of the different ways that you have made new friends. What did you do when you wanted to make a new friend? *(Ask volunteers to share their ideas. If children have difficulty getting started, you might need to provide a few examples such as you can ask the person to play with you, you can ask the person his/her name, or you can ask the person what kind of things he or she likes to do.)*

# Affirmation Jar

## Purpose:
Loneliness often stems from feelings of isolation and thinking that no one cares. This activity helps children recognize that they can gather emotional support by knowing that there are people who care about them and love them.

## Preparation Time: Several hours

## What You Need:
- Small containers with lids, one per child
- Fabric or construction paper
- Glue
- Glitter
- Who Loves Me? (page 236)
- Crayons and markers

## What to Do:
This activity encourages children to think about the people who love them. It is important to help children realize that there are many people who love them. These people can help the children through times when they are feeling lonely. During lonely times, the affirmation jar can be an enormous help to children.

Before this activity, collect and clean the containers for children to use. You may wish to make this a two-part activity, where the first step is to decorate the containers and the second step to draw the pictures to be placed in the containers. You may prefer to provide decorated containers depending on the skill level of the children you teach.

Reproduce the Who Loves Me? cards (page 236), making several copies for each child. To start the activity, give each child one copy. Ask the children to draw pictures of the people who love them. Point out that they should only draw one person on each card. Then help them write the name of each person they drew. Show children how to place the cards in their containers. Tell children that they can keep their affirmation jars at school or at home. Explain that they can look at the pictures whenever they wish, especially if they feel lonely.

## What to Say:
Today you are going to draw pictures of the people who love you. Let's talk about some of the people you know who love you. These people can be your mommies, daddies, brothers, sisters, aunts, uncles, cousins, grandparents, teachers, and friends. After you think about who loves you, let's draw a picture of each person. I will help everyone write each person's name on the picture. Then we will put the pictures in special containers. This way you will have the pictures to look at any time you feel lonely or just need to remember that many people love you.

# Who Loves Me?

# Class Book

## Purpose:

The purpose of this activity is to make children aware of some of the things they can do to help themselves when they feel lonely.

## Preparation Time: Half an hour

## What You Need:

- Three-ring binder
- When I Feel Lonely (page 238), one per child
- Crayons or markers
- Three-hole punch
- Binder Cover (page 239)

## What to Do:

Before this activity, reproduce and color the binder cover. Glue the cover onto the front of the binder. Reproduce page 238 and punch holes in the copies.

Begin this activity by talking to children about the things they do when they feel lonely. Ask them to share their experiences and discuss the kinds of things that help them when they feel lonely. Then have children make pictures that show something they like to do when they are lonely. If they have stories they want to tell you about their pictures, write these on the pictures they make.

Then after the children have finished their pictures, give them time to share their pictures with the rest of the group. After the children have told about their pictures, invite them to add the completed pictures to the binder. The end result will be a book that can be added to your classroom library. Children will enjoy looking at their book again and again.

## What to Say:

Today we are going to talk about what kinds of things you like to do when you feel lonely. For example, I like to sit in my backyard and watch birds fly from tree to tree. There's one bird that comes every day, and my family has named it Tweet. It's fun to sit quietly by myself and watch Tweet.

Now, let's talk about the some things that you do when you feel lonely. *(Allow time for children to share their ideas. Accept all suggestions.)* Now I want you to pick one way you help yourself feel better when you are lonely. Draw a picture of yourself doing that. When everyone is done, you will share your pictures. Then I will put them into a binder to make a class book. You can read our class book again and again. I hope this will help you think of things you can do the next time you feel lonely.

# When I Feel Lonely

When I feel lonely, I

_____

- - - - - - - - - - - - - - - - - - - - - - - - - - - -

_____

_____

- - - - - - - - - - - - - - - - - - - - - - - - - - - -

_____

- - - - - - - - - - - - - - - - - - - - - - - - - - - -

_____

- - - - - - - - - - - - - - - - - - - - - - - - - - - -

_____

# Binder Cover

# Illness

## Section Introduction

Everyone Gets Sick (page 241)

## Story

"Getting Better" (pages 242–251)

This story is about being sick and getting better. It provides youngsters with an inside look at a hospital and the helpful people who work there.

## Stick Puppet and Flannelboard Patterns

These patterns (pages 252–260) can be used to help children understand the issues that are emphasized in the story.

## Activities

- Doctor's Office/Hospital Tour (pages 261–263)
- Doll Hospital Center (pages 265–270)
- Classroom First Aid Kit (page 271)
- Emergency Telephone Game (pages 272–274)
- Get Well Gift (pages 275 and 276)

All of these activities provide children with information about illness so they can better cope with this problem. They also help alleviate some of the fears children have about illness.

# Everyone Gets Sick

Illness is a fact of life for children and adults. Even in countries that have excellent health care regulations and facilities, children become ill. Some must learn to cope with their own chronic, debilitating, or terminal illnesses. Other children are deeply affected by the health problems of those they love. Many aspects of illness are very frightening to children. Serious illnesses can separate children from their parents, they may be painful, or they can require painful treatments. What can educators do to help children who are affected by illness?

## Providing Information

As is true with anything that is not understood, illness is always more frightening to children when they lack information about it. Teachers can help reduce the anxiety children feel about illness by honestly and carefully providing this type of information at a level they can understand. It is important to familiarize children with the tools that doctors and hospitals use and explain, as much as possible, some general medical procedures that might take place. For example, children could use stethoscopes to listen to each other's heartbeats. Explain to children that for safety reasons, they can only use these for their intended purpose. You may wish to invite a medical professional to help you provide information about a specific illness with which a child in your class is having to cope.

## Framing the Truth Responsibly

Teachers need to be sure they do not tell children that painful procedures or treatments will not hurt. It is essential to tell children about the procedure/treatment so they will know what to expect. Point out any positive outcomes that may result from it. For example, inoculations are painful. However, they are important because they protect children from diseases, and they are needed in order for children to attend school without infecting others. An important but difficult task for educators is helping youngsters see the cause-and-effect relationships of illness.

## In This Book

This book provides a variety of suggestions to help children deal with experiences relating to illness. The section begins with a story about hospitals (pages 242–251), giving even very young children some basic information about what they will find there. Stick puppet and flannel board patterns (pages 252–260) are provided for children to role-play the story as well as their own experiences, fears, and expectations. Activities (pages 261–276) are included to help children understand and cope with illness.

# Getting Better

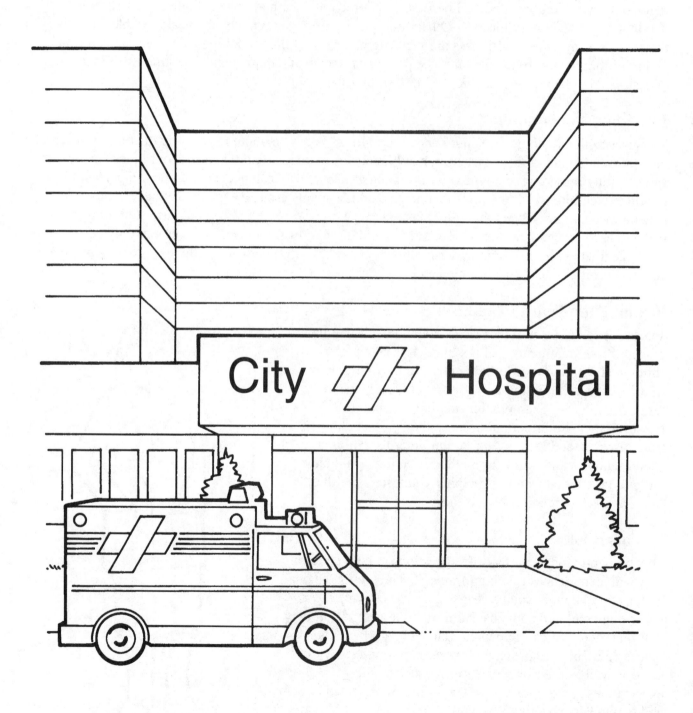

Sometimes people get very sick, and they must go to a hospital.

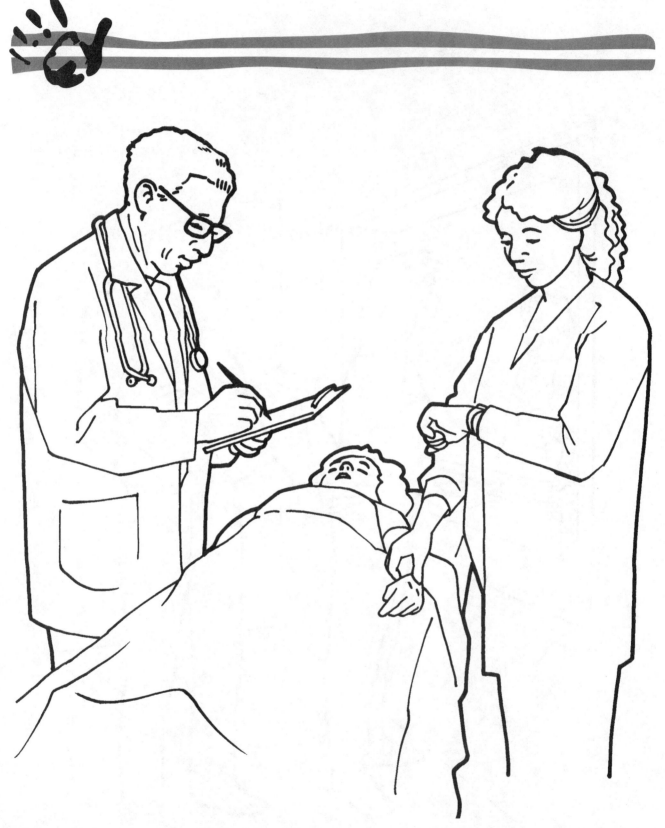

Hospitals are places where doctors and nurses work. Doctors and nurses take care of people who are sick and help them get better.

People in a hospital stay in bed and wear special hospital gowns.

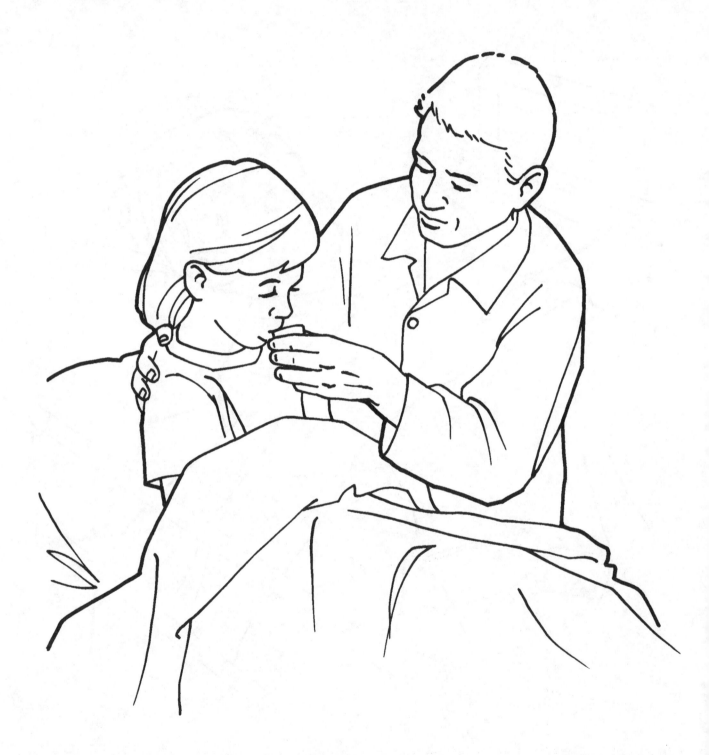

Many hospital patients must take medicine to help them feel better.

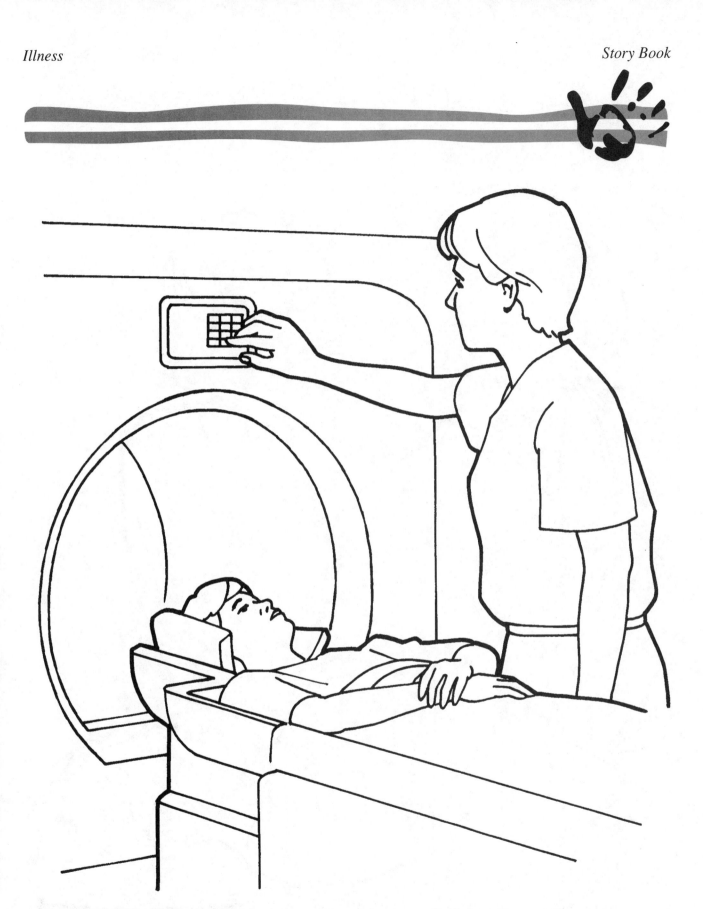

People in a hospital may have special tests using strange looking machines. These tests help doctors find out why they are sick.

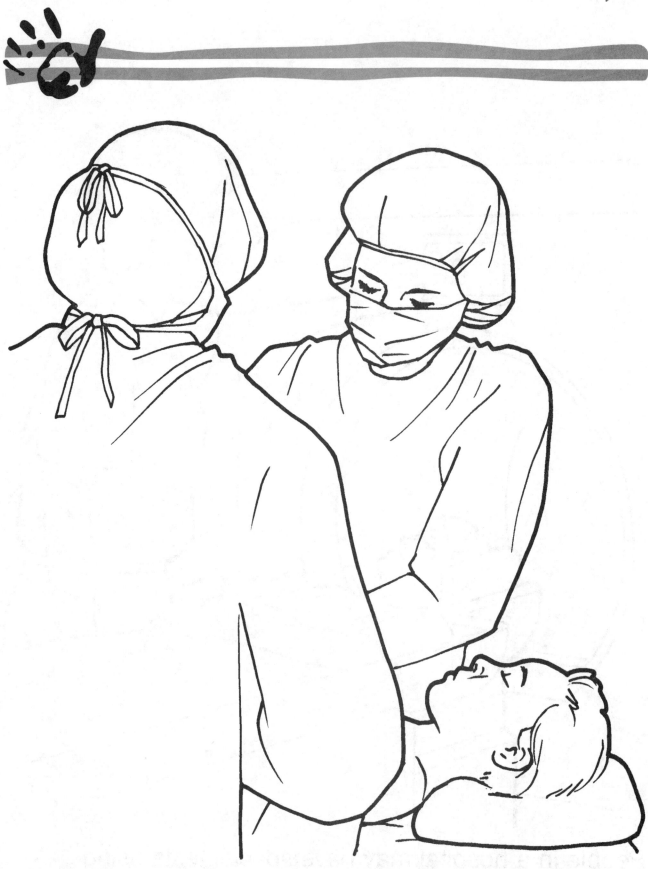

Sometimes people in a hospital have surgery. This means they have operations.

When sick people go to a hospital, their friends and family may come to visit. The visitors often bring gifts such as flowers, cards, games, toys, and other things to cheer up the people who are staying in the hospital.

Most people will get better while they are in a hospital.
Soon they will be well enough to go home.

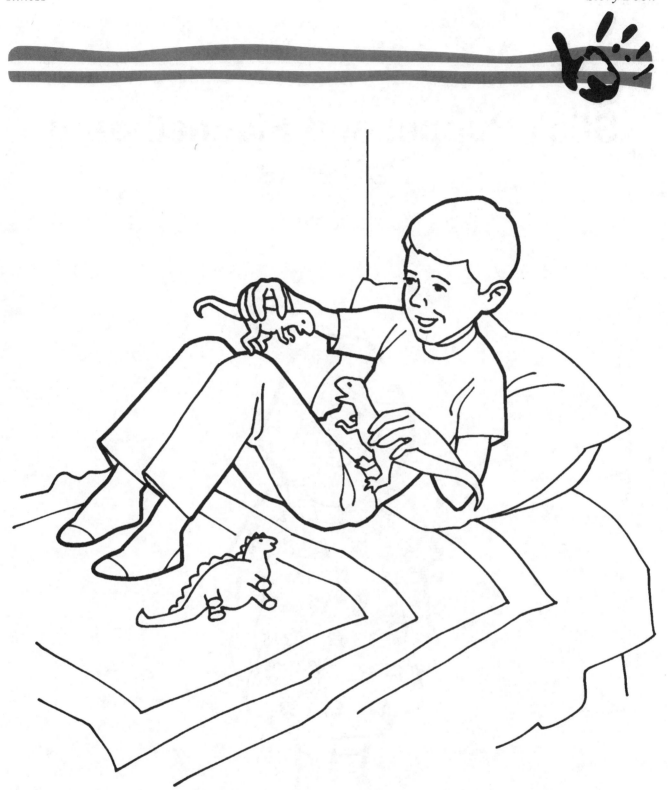

People who have been in a hospital will be glad to be home again. But they will still need to get plenty of rest and do what their doctors tell them. Then they can get completely better.

# Stick Puppet and Flannelboard Patterns

## Sick Girl

# Stick Puppet and Flannelboard Patterns *(cont.)*

## Sick Boy

# Stick Puppet and Flannelboard
# Patterns *(cont.)*

**Male Nurse**

# Stick Puppet and Flannelboard Patterns *(cont.)*

**Female Nurse**

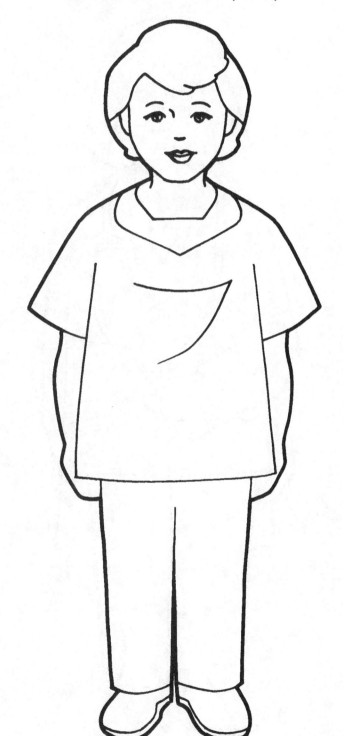

# Stick Puppet and Flannelboard Patterns *(cont.)*

**Female Doctor**

# Stick Puppet and Flannelboard Patterns *(cont.)*

**Male Doctor**

# Stick Puppet and Flannelboard
# Patterns *(cont.)*

## Various Hospital Equipment

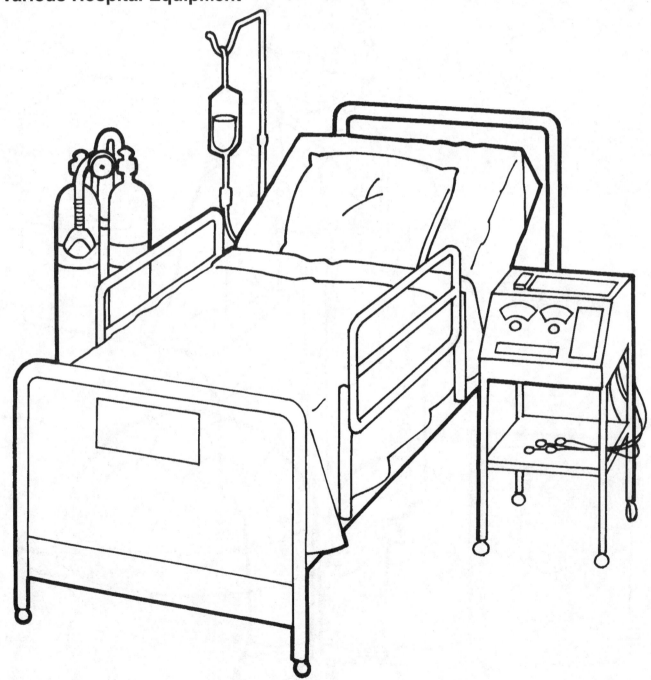

# Stick Puppet and Flannelboard Patterns *(cont.)*

**Flowers, Card, Toy, and Present**

# Stick Puppet and Flannelboard Patterns *(cont.)*

## Wheelchair

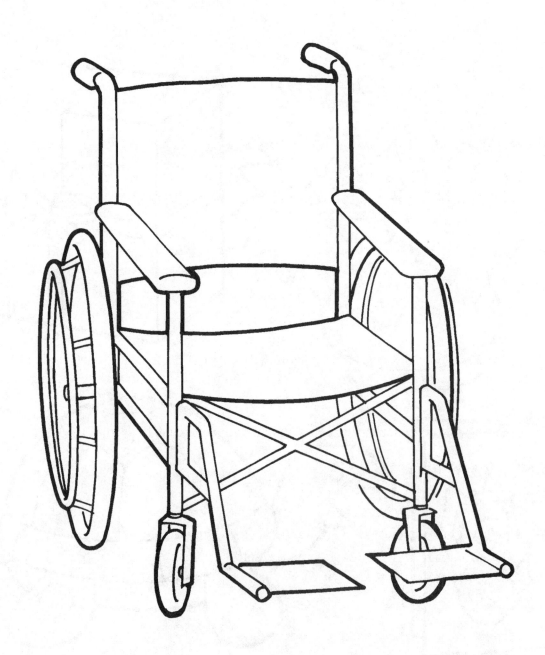

# Doctor's Office or Hospital Tour

## Purpose:

This activity allows children to become familiar with medical settings, such as a doctor's office or a hospital, and the people who work there. By doing this children should be less fearful when they are sick and have to go to a doctor or hospital.

**Preparation Time:** Several hours

## What You Need:

- Permission Slip (page 262)
- Hospital/Doctor Letter (page 264)
- Parent Volunteer Form (page 263)

## What to Do:

A field trip to a local hospital or doctor's office gives children a chance to see these environments in a friendly, non-threatening way. Obtain parent permission using the form on page 262.

Before beginning this activity with the children, select a medical facility you would like the children to tour. Use the letter provided on page 264 to contact the facility and arrange a date and time for the visit. If a parent of one of your students is a doctor or nurse, this may be easier to arrange.

Begin this activity by discussing illness with children. Read the story "Getting Better" (pages 242–251) as an introduction. Encourage children to share their experiences with illness. Then explain to them that they will have an opportunity to tour a doctor's office and/or a hospital. Point out that they will get to meet the nurses and doctors. You may wish to have children brainstorm some questions they want to ask the medical personnel.

Be sure to cover the following ideas/concepts with children before the field trip:

- Appropriate field trip behavior
- What they might see at the medical facility
- Rules for staying together with a buddy and the class
- Things they might be interested in asking the doctor(s), nurse(s), or technician(s)
- Use the letter on page 263 to ask for parent volunteers to help with this field trip as well as other classroom class activities

## What to Say:

We are going to visit a real hospital/doctor's office so we can see what it is really like. Let's talk about the kinds of things we might see in a hospital/doctor's office. *(Lead a discussion.)* Now let's talk about how we should behave when we visit the hospital/doctor's office. *(Encourage children to determine what type of behavior is appropriate while on a field trip.)*

# **Permission Slip**

Date _____

Dear Parent(s),

As part of our unit on illness, we are learning about doctors' offices and hospitals. We are planning the following field trip to extend our learning beyond the classroom.

Name of Doctor or Hospital: _____

Address: _____

Date: _____ Time: _____

Please sign this permission slip, and have your child return it by _____.
On the day of the field trip, please have your child bring:_____

_____.

I am looking for parent volunteers to accompany us on this trip. Please call if you are interested in joining us or if you have any questions.

Sincerely,

_____
Teacher

_____
School

_____
Telephone

---------------------------------------------------------------------------------

Child's Name: _____

       ❏ My child has permission to go on the field trip.

Parent's Signature: _____ Date: _____

# Parent Volunteer Form

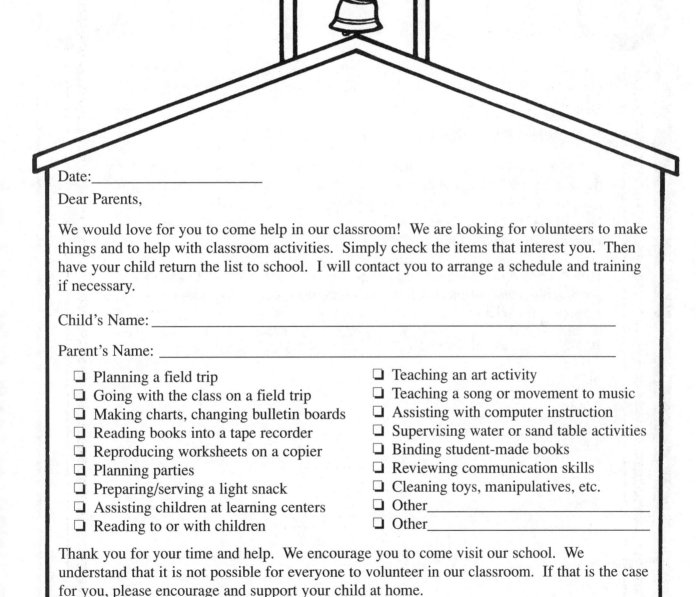

Date:_____

Dear Parents,

We would love for you to come help in our classroom! We are looking for volunteers to make things and to help with classroom activities. Simply check the items that interest you. Then have your child return the list to school. I will contact you to arrange a schedule and training if necessary.

Child's Name: _____

Parent's Name: _____

❏ Planning a field trip
❏ Going with the class on a field trip
❏ Making charts, changing bulletin boards
❏ Reading books into a tape recorder
❏ Reproducing worksheets on a copier
❏ Planning parties
❏ Preparing/serving a light snack
❏ Assisting children at learning centers
❏ Reading to or with children

❏ Teaching an art activity
❏ Teaching a song or movement to music
❏ Assisting with computer instruction
❏ Supervising water or sand table activities
❏ Binding student-made books
❏ Reviewing communication skills
❏ Cleaning toys, manipulatives, etc.
❏ Other_____
❏ Other_____

Thank you for your time and help. We encourage you to come visit our school. We understand that it is not possible for everyone to volunteer in our classroom. If that is the case for you, please encourage and support your child at home.

Sincerely,

Teacher:_____

School: _____

Phone:_____

# Hospital/Doctor Letter

Date:_____

Dear Medical Professional_____,

Our class is completing a unit about illness. In it, I am teaching children about doctors' offices and hospitals so they will feel more comfortable when they have to see doctors or other medical professionals. To extend our learning beyond the classroom, I would like to take my class to a doctor's office or other medical facility for a brief visit.

I am interested in having the children tour your facility and would like to speak with you about the possibility of arranging this. If a class tour is possible, please let me know a convenient time for us to come visit and if there are any special rules or requirements I need to be aware of before bringing the children to your facility. Thank you in advance for your help.

Sincerely,

_____
Teacher

_____
School

_____
Phone

# Doll Hospital Center

## Purpose:
This activity gives children a chance to role-play being doctors and nurses in a Doll Hospital Center. They use stuffed animals and dolls for their patients.

## Preparation Time: One afternoon

## What You Need:
- Shoe boxes
- Stuffed animals and dolls
- Posterboard
- Masking tape
- Glue
- Tissue
- Patient's Chart (page 266)
- Doctor's Hat (page 267)
- Doctor's Bag (page 268)
- Stethoscope (page 269)
- Medical Equipment (page 270)
- Laminating film or clear contact paper (optional)

## What to Do:
Begin this activity by determining a place for the Doll Hospital Center in your classroom. It is very possible to put this center together in one afternoon with little or no cost, using materials you already have on hand. Decide ahead of time if you will provide the dolls and stuffed animals to be the patients or if children will bring their own.

Then reproduce the Patient's Chart (page 266) and Medical Equipment (page 270). Glue the equipment patterns onto poster board. Laminate them or cover them with clear contact paper. Have each child make a Doctor's Hat, Doctor's Bag, and Stethoscope (pages 267–269) to use in the center. Have children use the shoe boxes for the patients' beds and the tape and tissue for bandages.

Use the story "Getting Better" (pages 242–251) to introduce the activity, or begin by asking children to share their own experiences with doctors and hospitals.

## What to Say:
I have made a new center for our classroom. It is a Doll Hospital Center. You can use this center when you pretend to be doctors and nurses. Your patients will be the dolls and stuffed animals. It will be your job to take care of your sick patients. *(Discuss with children what is in the center.)*

# Patient's Chart

Patient's Name: _____

# Doctor's Hat

Use the following directions for each doctor's hat.

1. Reproduce the pattern onto poster board.  Cut out the pattern.
2. Cover the poster board with aluminum foil.
3. Measure and cut a 4" (10.5 cm) wide band of tagboard.  The length will vary depending on the size of the child's head.
4. Use glue to connect the circle to the front of the band.
5. Tape or staple the band to fit the child's head.

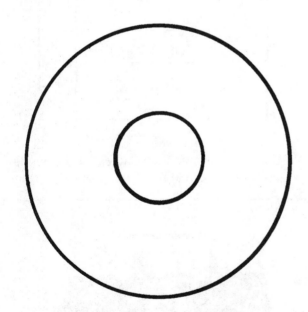

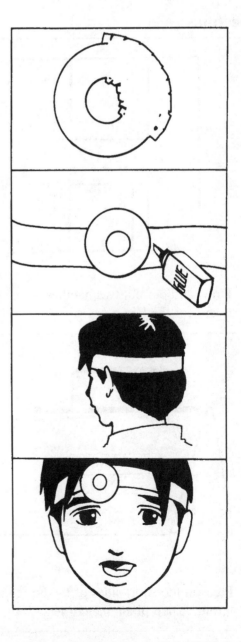

# Doctor's Bag

Use the following directions to make a medical bag, such as those carried by doctors.

## Materials:

- Shoe box
- Scissors
- Black tempera paint

- Poster board
- Stapler
- Paintbrush

## Directions:

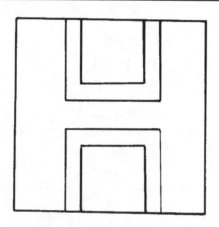

1. Draw and cut out two handles from poster board for the bag.

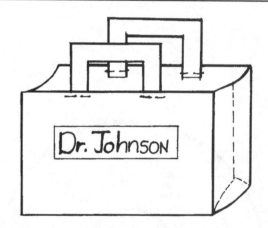

2. Center and staple the handles onto the long sides of the shoe box in the middle.

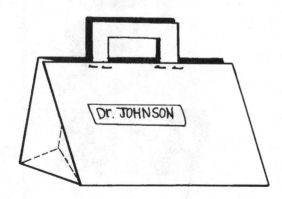

3. Press in the short sides of the box to make a fold. Then pinch the corners.

4. Paint the box and handles black with tempera paint. Allow the paint to dry.

# Stethoscope

Use the following directions to make a stethoscope.

## Materials:

- Plastic hose
- Funnel

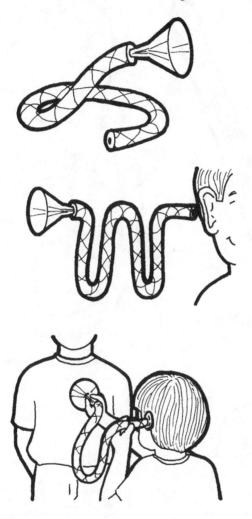

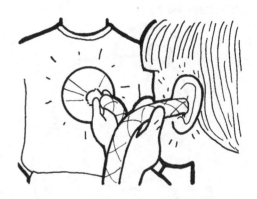

## Directions:

1. Connect the plastic hose to the funnel.

2. Place the other end of the plastic hose in your ear.

3. Place the funnel on a friend's chest.

4. Listen to your friend's heart beat.

5. Place the funnel on your chest and listen to your own heart beat.

6. Use your stethoscope when you play in the Doll Hospital Center.

# Medical Equipment

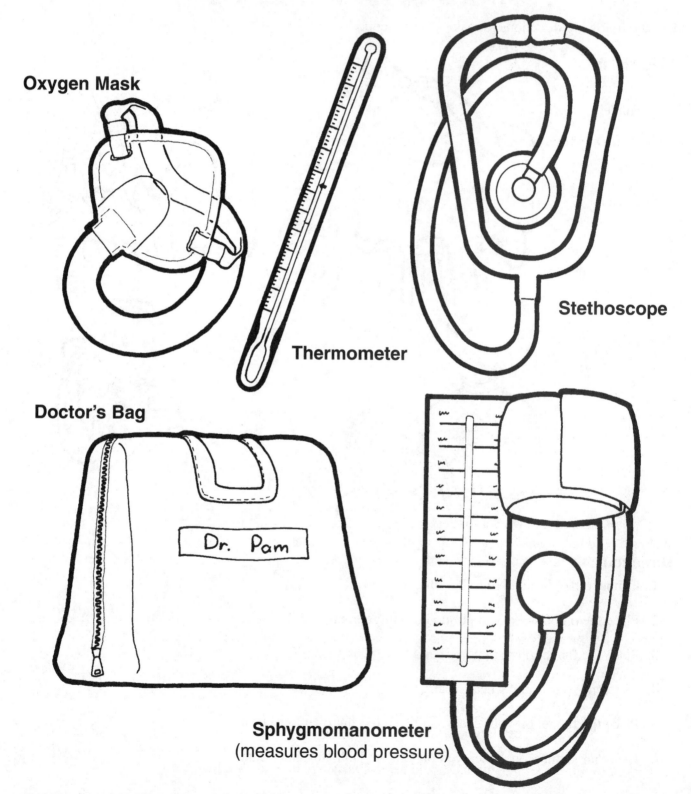

**Oxygen Mask**

**Thermometer**

**Stethoscope**

**Doctor's Bag**

Dr. Pam

**Sphygmomanometer**
(measures blood pressure)

# Classroom First-Aid Kit

**Purpose:**

This activity gives children an opportunity to help make a classroom first aid kit and learn about what to do in the case of minor classroom accidents.

**Preparation Time:** One afternoon

**What You Need:**

- Antiseptic
- Adhesive bandages, different sizes
- Sterile gauze pads, different sizes
- Adhesive tape
- Syrup of ipecac
- Small pair of scissors
- Tweezers
- Plastic gloves
- Large plastic container with tightly fitting lid
- Emergency Numbers (page 273)

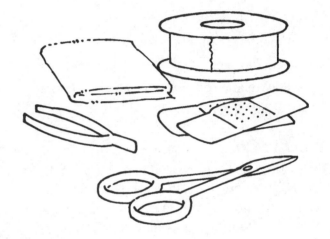

**What to Do:**

In this activity, children will have the opportunity to make a first aid kit that you will be able to use in your classroom. Before beginning this activity with your class, gather the necessary materials. You will need a large plastic container with a tightly fitting lid to make the kit. Then decide what supplies you think are necessary for the first aid kit and buy them or obtain them from the school nurse. Some basic items are suggested above in What You Need.

Explain to the children what a first aid kit is. Ask them to tell what happens at home when they get hurt and let them brainstorm a list of supplies they think are important to have in a first aid kit. (You may wish to use this portion of the activity to help you to determine what will go into the first aid kit.)

**What to Say:**

What should you do when you fall down and scrape your knees or get a cut on your finger? If you are at home, you probably tell your mother or father. What does your mother or father do? *(Invite volunteers to respond.)* What can you do to help yourself? *(Talk about first aid procedures that children are capable of doing for themselves. For example, they can wash a cut, get an adhesive bandage, etc.)* One day you might get a cut or scrape at school, so we need to be ready to take care of those little accidents. To do this, we are going to make a first aid kit. Let's talk about what kinds of things we want to have in it and why we need them. *(Lead a discussion about the types of supplies that should be in a first aid kit and why each item is important to have on hand in a classroom.)* It is important to remember that adults should always take care of medical situations.

# Emergency Telephone Game

## Purpose:

This activity prepares children for an emergency by teaching them how to dial a phone to summon help. It also allows children to become familiar with their own phone numbers and addresses.

## Preparation Time: One hour

## What You Need:

- Emergency Numbers (page 273)
- Pencil or pen
- Play phones or disconnected real phones
- Parent Letter (page 274)

## What to Do:

Every child needs to be able to dial a phone in case of an emergency. In order to do this, they need instruction as well as opportunities to practice. In this activity, you can help children gain practical experience so they will know what to do during an emergency.

Before beginning this activity, gather the materials you need. It is important to have children memorize their phone numbers and addresses. Be sure they understand when it is appropriate to dial 911 or 0 for help. Let them use a play phone or a disconnected real phone to ensure that they understand how it operates.

## What to Say:

It is very important to know what to do if you have an emergency. First, let's talk about emergencies. Can anyone tell me what an emergency is? *(Repeatedly reinforce the concept of an emergency. Help children differentiate between small problems and true emergencies. It is often difficult for young children to understand what an emergency is.)*

If you have an emergency, and you need the police, fire fighters, or an ambulance you should dial 911. Today you are going to learn how to dial 911 or 0 and ask for help. Be sure you dial 911 only when someone is hurt and you don't have an adult to help you. For example, if I fell down and hurt myself, I would need you to get help for me. *(Allow children to suggest other emergency scenarios that could arise. Demonstrate how to dial 911 or 0 and how to provide the necessary information. Allow time for each child to practice.)*

# EMERGENCY NUMBERS

## Dial **911** or **0** for the operator!

Or you can call the...

**Fire Department:** _____

**Police Department:** _____

**Hospital:** _____

**Poison Control Center:** _____

# Parent Letter

Date:_____

Dear Parents,

As part of our unit on illness, we are learning about accidents and what to do during an emergency. We have discussed what an emergency is and when it is appropriate to call 911 or 0 for help. The children have practiced dialing 911 or 0 and giving pertinent information such as their phone numbers and addresses. Please review the safety information your child has learned at school.

A list of emergency phone numbers is attached. Ask your child to help you post these numbers near your telephone. Use the following suggestions to prepare your child for an emergency.

- Discuss with your child what kinds of things (cleaning fluids, plants, gasoline, paints, etc.) are poisons in your home. Show your child some examples of these. Stress how dangerous these items are. Then be sure these items are placed out of the child's reach.
- Talk about kitchen safety rules.
- Use the back of this letter to draw an escape plan from your home in case there is a fire. Have fire drills to practice the escape plan. Be sure to stress the following to your child:

  1. Stay calm at all times.
  2. If smoke begins to fill the room, cover your mouth with your hand and crawl on the floor.
  3. If your clothes catch on fire, remember to **STOP, DROP, and ROLL.**
  4. Never open a door that feels hot.
  5. Run to the nearest telephone to report the fire by dialing **911** or **0** for the operator.

- Discuss how only an adult family member or a doctor should ever give your child any medicine.
- Take a walk around your home with your child. Find ways to make your home safer by correcting problems that could cause accidents, such as toys left on the floor, a wet bathroom floor, and too many appliances plugged into an outlet.

Sincerely,

_____

Teacher

_____

School

_____

Phone

# Get Well Gifts

**Purpose:**

This activity gives children an opportunity to make a bookmark for a friend or family member who is ill.

**Preparation Time:** One hour

**What You Need:**

- Bookmarks (page 276)
- Cardstock
- Crayons and markers
- Scissors
- Laminating film or clear contact paper
- One-hole punch
- Thin ribbon

**What to Do:**

Before beginning this activity, gather the materials together. You may wish to set up an Art Center so several children can work on making bookmarks at the same time. However, you may prefer to do this activity with the entire class.

Begin this activity by discussing get-well presents. Ask children what they could do or make to help a sick friend or family member feel better.

Reproduce the bookmarks onto cardstock. Have children color and decorate the bookmarks. Laminate the bookmarks or cover them with clear contact paper. Punch a hole at the top end of each bookmark and knot a piece of ribbon there.

**What to Say:**

When friends or family members are sick, you might be able to help cheer them up by making a present for them. A present also lets these people know that we are thinking about them and that we care about how they are feeling. There are many types of presents that you can give someone who is sick. Some presents are things that the sick person can use. Other presents are just nice to look at or fun to have. Today you are going to make a pretty and useful get-well gift—a bookmark. There are three different types of bookmarks to choose from. Choose one that you would like to decorate. After you have decorated your bookmark, I will help you tie a piece of ribbon on it. *(Allow children to choose bookmarks and decorate them. Then punch the hole and tie the ribbon onto each bookmark.)*

# Bookmarks

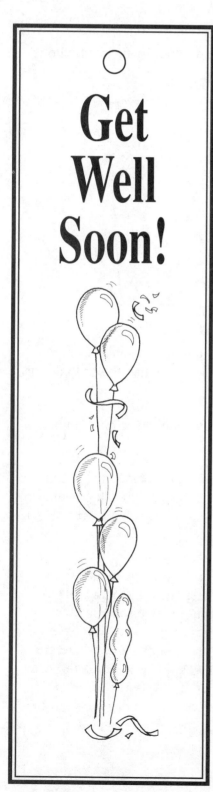

# Abuse

## Section Introduction

## Story

This rhyming story teaches children that they are in charge of their bodies and that they have the right to choose how they are touched and by whom.

## Stick Puppet and Flannelboard Patterns

These patterns (pages 291–294) can be used to help children understand the issues that are emphasized in the story.

## Activities

These activities deal with developing a positive self-concept, teaching abuse prevention by reinforcing children's right to set boundaries on touch for their own bodies, and helping children understand how to handle other living things with care.

# Children and Abuse

## Prevention Is Best

The issue of child abuse may be the leading health and safety issue of our times. It is crucial that children learn and understand rules that can help keep them safe. We must begin as soon as possible to teach children that they deserve respect and that they have the right to safeguard their emotional and physical integrity. We must be equally clear that this extends to everyone because most of the time it is someone the child knows and trusts who is the abuser.

We are all responsible for the children in our care and in our lives. It is up to us to provide safe environments for all children to the best of our ability. Even at a very young age, children can learn and understand safety rules. We must teach these rules to children with the same intent, caring, and calmness that we teach them to look both ways before they cross a street.

As with all health and safety concerns, prevention is best. Children need the truth, but not the whole truth. We do not tell them exactly what will happen to their fragile bodies if they get hit by a car. It is enough for them to know that we care about them and that we make these rules because we want them to stay safe and healthy. Children need for us to believe—and show them—that if we all do the best we can, then most of the time everything will be all right.

Children know that bad things happen. They know that everyone makes mistakes and that nobody is perfect. We must also acknowledge and accept this, for no matter how hard we try, we cannot protect any child all the time. But we can reassure children that most mistakes can be fixed, that bad things that happen to them are not their fault, and that they can come to us for help. Most of all, children need to know that no matter what, we love them and care for them.

## Reporting Suspected Abuse

It is the law that anyone who has reason to believe or suspect that a child has been abused physically, mentally, emotionally, or sexually report the situation to state and local law enforcement and to child protective services. Learn the legal requirements for reporting child abuse and neglect in your state. Even if nothing is done, it is crucial that the child's record reflect these suspicions in case of future incidents or complaints.

## In This Book

There are many facets to child abuse and its prevention. This section focuses on setting boundaries to stop unwanted touch. Even young children can learn that their bodies belong to them and that the word "No" means exactly that. Children must learn that touch is never a secret. Reproduce the information for parents (page 279) on how to appropriately nurture their children. The story in this section teaches children that they have the right to choose how they are touched and by whom (pages 280–290). Stick puppet and flannel board patterns (pages 291–294) are provided for children to role-play the story as well as their own experiences, fears, and concerns. Activities (pages 295–304) are included to help children learn abuse prevention strategies.

# For Parents

How would you answer these questions about your relationship with your child? You may wish to use the tips following the questions to strengthen your bond with your child.

1. Do I give my child encouragement and recognition?

   Say more positive things than negative things to your child. Don't label your child.

2. Do I take time to really listen and give my child my undivided attention?

   Acknowledge and take seriously your child's feelings, ideas, and emotions. Listen more than you talk, and don't belittle your child.

3. Do I take out my bad day, anger, or resentment on my child?

   Explain to your child when you are upset, and apologize if you do lash out inappropriately at him/her. Don't be afraid to say, "I'm sorry. I was wrong."

4. Do I treat my child with the same respect I would treat a friend?

   Have age-appropriate expectations for your child, and treat him/her as the valuable, loved person he/she is.

5. Do I allow my child to make mistakes and learn from them?

   Help your child understand that everyone makes mistakes and that most of them can be fixed. Help your child discover solutions for problems or for fixing mistakes.

6. Am I a good role model?

   Children learn most of their behavior from watching others. Express your values, and let your child know where you stand on things.

7. Do I discipline my child when I am angry?

   Set rules and be sure your child understands them, knows the limits for behavior, and is clear about the consequences. Wait until you are calm to discipline your child.

8. Do I take the time to play, work, and just be with my child?

   Show your child how much you care by spending time with him or her.

9. Do I tell my child "I love you" and give hugs generously?

   Be sure your child knows that you love him/her all the time, no matter what— even when you don't like your child's behavior.

10. Is my child's health and safety the most important thing to me?

    Learn as much as you can about how to help your child learn to protect himself or herself when you are not around.

# It's My Choice

You're my friends and family.

I love you, and you love me.

I like hugs and kisses, too.

And I like holding hands with you.

But I don't want touch all the time.

I want it when the choice is mine.

My body just belongs to me.

It's my choice to be safe and free.

282

Please don't hug me really tight.

That kind of touch does not feel right.

Please don't pinch or hit or shove.

That kind of touch does not show love.

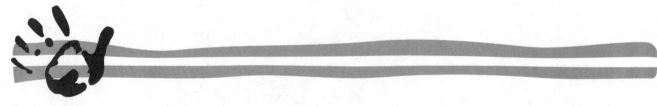

If I don't like or want your touch,

I'll say, "I don't like that much."

"Please don't touch me in that way."

And then I'll move your hand away.

If I say, "Stop," you might feel bad.

But I don't mean to make you mad.

Who touches me must be my choice.

To let you know, I'll use my voice.

If you don't stop, then I will yell.

I'll run away and get some help.

I'll tell a grown-up what you did.

It's my choice how you touch this kid.

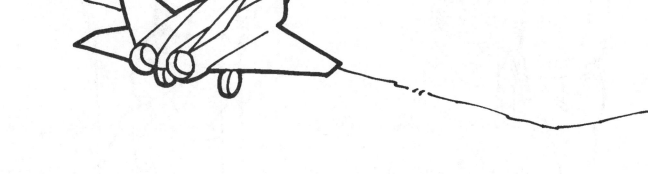

I'll do the same with strangers, too.

It really doesn't matter who.

What matters is that this is me.

My body, my choice. Do you see?

If I want touch, then it's just fine.

But I can always change my mind.

Sometimes I do, sometimes I don't.

Sometimes we'll touch, sometimes we won't.

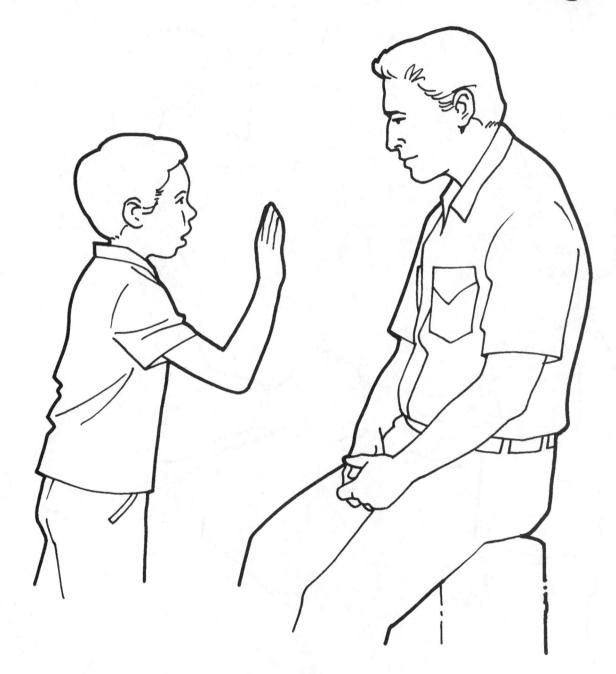

You are my friends and family.

And I love you, and you love me.

We can all let our love show

By stopping when someone says, "No."

I'll tell you what. Let's make a deal.

We'll tell each other how we feel.

I promise I'll treat you the way

I want you to treat me. Okay?

# Stick Puppet and Flannelboard Patterns

### Little Girls

# Stick Puppet and Flannelboard Patterns *(cont.)*

## Little Boys

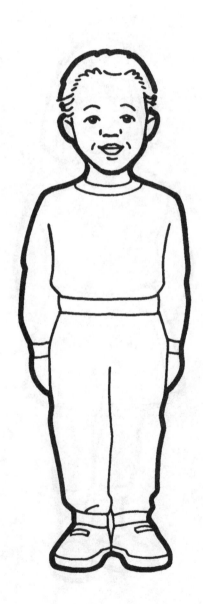
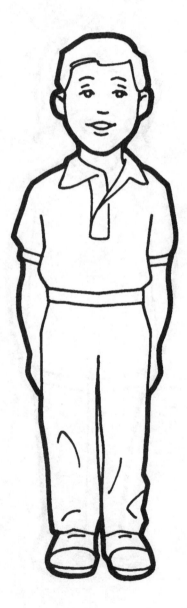

# Stick Puppet and Flannelboard Patterns *(cont.)*

## Adult Males

# Stick Puppet and Flannelboard Patterns *(cont.)*

## Adult Females

294

# Life-Size Self-Portrait

## Purpose:

The purpose of this activity is to help children develop positive self-concepts since this is the first step in abuse prevention.

## Preparation Time: One hour

## What You Need:

- Butcher paper or poster board, one piece per child
- Large tipped marker
- Crayons or markers
- Scissors
- Glue
- Yarn (optional)
- Fabric remnants (optional)
- Ribbon (optional)

## What to Do:

Clear a large space on the floor and have a child lie down on a large sheet of butcher paper or poster board. Then trace around the child with a large tipped marker. If you would like to do more than one child's outline at a time, enlist the help of parent volunteers or older students for this activity.

You may wish to give the children a variety of art materials to create their self-portraits. However, it is possible for them to do the whole activity using only crayons or markers. As an alternative, you may wish to provide yarn for hair and fabric remnants and ribbon for clothing.

Hang the finished products on the classroom walls. Encourage children to tell what is special about themselves.

## What to Say:

Today you are going to make pictures of yourself that are the same size you are. First, you will lie down on a piece of butcher paper/poster board. *(Invite a volunteer to lay down on a piece of butcher paper/poster board.)* Then I will trace the outline of your body. *(Trace the child's outline onto the butcher paper/poster board.)* This is what it will look like. *(Show children the outline.)* After I have drawn your outline, you will get to color and decorate your self-portrait. When everyone is finished coloring and decorating, you will get to show us your self-portrait and tell how you are special.

# Setting Boundaries

## Purpose:

The purpose of these activities is to help children learn that they have the right to their bodies and "personal space"; how to judge when someone is getting too close, i.e., intruding their personal space; how to use their voices and bodies to set boundaries; how to stop unwanted touch.

## Preparation Time: One hour

## What You Need:

- Touch I Like (page 299)          • Touch I Don't Like (page 300)

## What to Do and Say:

### Personal Space

Introduce the concept of personal space.

1. Ask children to stand in pairs and face their partners as if they are going to talk to each other.
2. After they have moved to be with their partners, have them "freeze."
3. Point out to children their "personal space" body language—how close they are to their partners.
4. Use one pair as an example and elicit from the partners if they are comfortable with how close they are to each other. Discuss with the class how people feel about being close to others. Do we all feel the same about being close to friends, family, and strangers? Are there differences? What might those differences be?
5. Discuss personal space and the right of each person to his/her body and a certain amount of space around him/her.
6. Discuss ways people can keep other people from invading their personal space (moving away, putting out a hand as a barrier, asking the person to not stand so close, etc.)

### Space Invaders

Divide the class into two lines that are facing each other. Have one line be "space invaders" and the other line be the "space patrol." At your signal, have the space invaders walk slowly toward the space patrol, and have the space patrol put up an outstretched hand as a "Stop" sign and strongly say "STOP" when they feel the invader is getting too close. Instruct the invaders to stop when they see the "stop sign" and respect the wishes of the space patrol. Reverse the roles so each child gets to be an invader and a patrol. Talk about what it felt like as the invader and the patrol.

# Setting Boundaries *(cont.)*

### *Please Do Not Touch*

Have the children sit cross-legged in a circle on the floor so they are close enough to touch each other's knees. Have the first child (the toucher) touch (lay his/her hand on) the knee of the child to his/her right. Have the touched child (touchee) do the following:

1. Make eye contact with the toucher.
2. Say aloud, "Please don't touch me," or "Please take your hand off my knee," or some other phrase that lets the toucher know that it is unwanted touch.

Have the toucher respect the child's request and remove his/her hand. Go around the circle with each child being a toucher and a touchee. Discuss with children that people who care about them will respect their boundaries on touch.

Also discuss with children that sometimes people don't listen, so you must get their attention. Go around the circle again, but this time have the toucher ignore the first request. (He/She does NOT remove his/her hand when asked.) Have the touchee use voice and body to stop the touch. This time, the touchee should do the following:

1. Make eye contact.
2. Make the request.
3. When the request is ignored, he/she should take his/her own hand and move the toucher's hand off his/her knee while saying, "I said stop."
   The toucher keeps his/her hand off.

Discuss with the class how it feels to be the touchee and the toucher. Talk about what they learned in the story they can do if someone does not listen to them (yell, go get help from an adult).

# Setting Boundaries (cont.)

### *Telling—Getting Help from an Adult*

Tell children that you will support their right to not be touched if they do not want to be touched, (unless an adult must touch them to stop them from hurting themselves or another person or causing property damage). Lead the class in a discussion of the importance of telling the whole story—exactly what happened. For example a child could say, "Ted keeps touching me and won't stop even when I ask him to" instead of, "Ted keeps bothering me."

Give children a pretend situation and have each one practice telling you the whole story about what happened. Reinforce that telling to stop a hurtful behavior (as opposed to tattling, or telling just to get someone in trouble) is a good thing to do by reassuring each child. For example, you could say, "I'm glad you told me about this. I'll take care of it right away. You did the right thing."

## Emphasize to children that touch is never a secret.

Talk to children about who they love and trust to help them. Tell children that if someone does not believe them, that it will make them feel bad, but they have the right to get help to stop unwanted touch. They need to keep telling more adults until someone believes them. Invite children to brainstorm a list of adults in their lives that they could go to to tell about unwanted touch.

# Touch I Like

I like_____.

# Touch I Don't Like

I don't like _____.

# Egg-Babies

## Purpose:
The purpose of this activity is to show children how to be gentle and kind. Young children have to learn kindness and gentleness. This activity gives them the opportunity to become more aware of their physical behavior and what it feels like to be gentle with something.

## Preparation Time: One afternoon

## What You Need:

- Raw eggs, one per child
- Clean yogurt cups, one per child
- Cotton balls, 10 per child
- One black permanent marker
- Clean-up supplies such as paper towels
- Egg-Baby Participation Certificate (page 302)
- Egg-Baby Award (page 303)
- Prizes for all participants (optional)

## What to Do:
Young children must learn what gentleness is. Prepare for this activity by getting an egg-baby and an egg-baby bed ready for each child. To create each egg-baby, simply use the black permanent marker to draw a cute face on the egg. To make each egg-baby bed, place several cotton balls inside a clean, empty yogurt cup. Put the egg-baby inside the cup.

Discuss gentleness. Ask children to suggest situations in which it is important to be gentle. Before doing the egg-baby activity, explain it to the children. Point out that the idea is for each child in the class to care of his or her own egg-baby throughout the day. This will help demonstrate how important it is to be gentle and careful with all living things. At the end of the day, give awards (page 302) to the children whose egg-babies have not been broken. Children can color the egg-baby faces on their participation certificates (page 302).

## What to Say:
We are going to play a game called the egg-baby game. Here is what we will do. First I will give each of you an egg-baby in a special egg-baby bed. Egg-babies are very easy to break so you must be careful when you touch them. Be sure you do not drop your egg-babies or they will break. Can anybody tell me what the egg-baby really is? That's right. It's an egg. We are going to pretend for the day that our egg-babies are real babies. We are going to keep them with us all day while we work and play. Remember, if you drop your egg-baby it will break. It will also break if you play roughly with it, if you throw it, or if you hug it too tightly. At the end of the day, we will see who still has an egg-baby that hasn't broken. Everyone will get a prize and participation certificate just for trying to be a good mommy or daddy for the day.

# Egg-Baby Participation Certificate

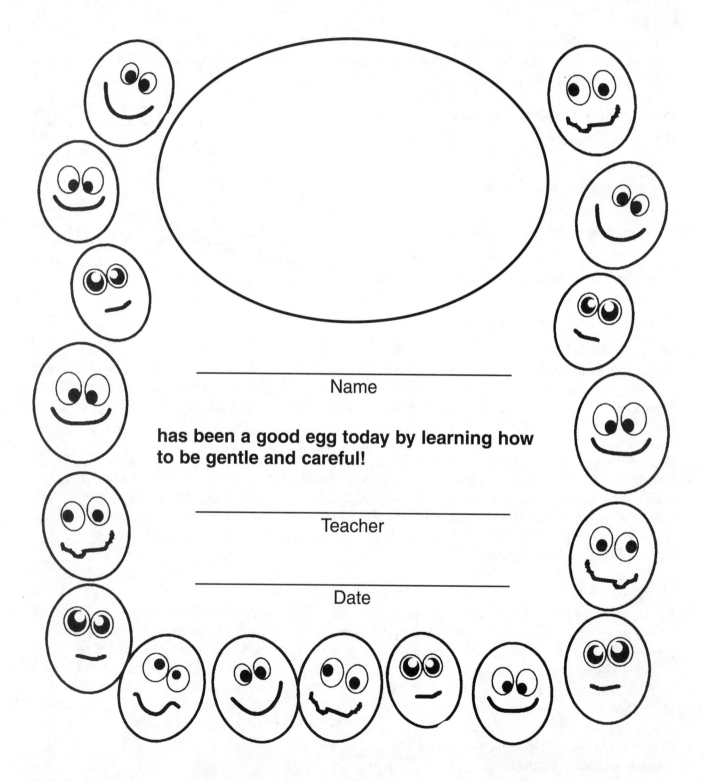

_____

Name

**has been a good egg today by learning how to be gentle and careful!**

_____

Teacher

_____

Date

# Egg-Baby Award

_____

## has shown
## Gentleness, Love, and Kindness
## to the Egg-Baby!

| | |
|---|---|
| _____ | _____ |
| Teacher | Date |

# How to Treat a Pet

**Purpose:**

In this activity children learn about pet care and responsibility using stuffed animals.

**Preparation Time:** One afternoon

**What You Need:**

- One or more stuffed dogs and/or cats
- Pet dishes
- New pet toys
- Leashes
- Collars
- Pet beds or blankets
- Brushes

**What to Do:**

In this activity, you create a Pet Care Center for children to make-believe that they are caring for their pets. It allows them to undertake the responsibilities of having pets while learning how to treat other living creatures with care.

Before this activity, talk to children about having pets. Mention to them that it is important to be able to practice caring for pets so they can do the best job possible. Point out that it will be fun pretending that stuffed animals are pets. During this explanation, show the children the stuffed pets. Have the class vote on names for the stuffed animals.

Then ask children what they know about each piece of pet equipment (brush, collar, bed, etc.). Model how to use each item or allow children to demonstrate. Encourage children to play with the stuffed animals in the Pet Care Center.

**What to Say:**

We have some new visitors to our classroom. They are stuffed animals, but we are going to pretend that they are our pets. You are going to take care of these pets just as if they were real. That way you can practice so you can do the best job possible of taking care of your real pets. If you don't have a pet, some day you might get one. Then it will be very important for you to know how to care for your pet. *(Use a variety of questions, such as those that follow, to prompt a discussion.)* Can anyone tell me how to take good care of a dog or cat? What special things do we need to do? What other kinds of pets do you have or would you like to have? How would you need to care for these animals?